SOME THOUGHTS
ON FAITH HEALING

EDITED BY VINCENT EDMUNDS
AND C. GORDON SCORER

CHRISTIAN MEDICAL FELLOWSHIP PUBLICATIONS
LONDON

© Christian Medical Fellowship, 1979

First Edition   1956
Second Edition   1966
Third Edition (extensively revised) 1979

Vincent Edmunds, M.D., F.R.C.P., is Consultant Physician, Mount Vernon Hospital, Northwood and the Mildmay Mission Hospital; and C. Gordon Scorer, M.B.E., M.D., F.R.C.S., was formerly Consultant Surgeon, Hillingdon Hospital, Middlesex, and Southall-Norwood Hospital.

Price £1.00

ISBN 0 85111 919 0

Made and printed in Great Britain by
Stanley L. Hunt (Printers) Ltd. Rushden Northamptonshire

CONTENTS

CONTENTS

PREFACE

The following pages originated in, and grew from, notes compiled during monthly meetings of a Study Group of Christian doctors in the years 1954 and 1955. Those taking part included consultants and senior registrars who represented most of the main branches of medical practice. Their original findings, revised and enlarged, were published in 1956 under the title *Some Thoughts on Faith Healing*. In response to many requests, the booklet was considerably revised and published again in 1966.

This 1979 edition differs from its predecessors in several respects. Some of the earlier contents have been omitted and the rest rearranged and up-dated. Additional material has been brought in from more recent studies, reports and publications. Chapter I will make clear the method of approach which it is hoped is more in keeping with the contemporary outlook in both Medicine and the Church.

Doctors have a particular interest in this subject because of their training and experience in the science and art of healing. As the patient tells his story they have to learn to differentiate the true from the false, the relevant from the irrelevant. They need to be critical of themselves and to be wary of prejudging issues. They have a duty, too, to make an objective assessment of those remedies which are suspected to be of doubtful value. Such judgments cannot usually be made quickly but need careful follow-up.

In recent years the subject of Faith Healing has become a very large one. To consider it in depth—including all the historical, theological, scientific and more popular backgrounds—would require a great deal more time than has been available to us or our colleagues. It would also need a large volume for its presentation. This however would defeat the needs of those—the majority being busy medical practitioners—who have requested a *short* practical survey of the present position. For any who desire to pursue particular aspects of special interest to them, the bibliography (page 98) has been compiled in order to indicate some of the chief authorities. We have also mentioned at various points in the text those studies which we believe to be the ablest and most relevant to the points discussed.

In theological outlook the original Study Group accepted the main positions of the historic Ecumenical Creeds and Reformed Confessions of Faith, and the present editors retain the same point of view. In particular they believe that God has revealed Himself personally in Jesus Christ, God the Son, and that He has made His will adequately and reliably known in Holy Scripture. It is their conviction that God has both the authority and the power to intervene by miracle at any time in the world which He has made.

This booklet brings together the edited comments of many professional colleagues and friends with whom we have met to discuss the question of Faith Healing over the years. The members of the original Study Group were: Dr. D. Martyn Lloyd-Jones (Chairman), Dr. Vincent Edmunds, Dr. Ronald E. D. Markillie, Mr. C. Gordon Scorer, Dr. David S. Short, Dr. Duncan W. Vere, Dr. S. Morgan Whitteridge and Dr. Douglas Johnson.   Dr. Johnson acted as Secretary to the Group, and, as in so many other things, his contributions over the years have been incalculable.   It is true to say that without his help this booklet would not have been published.   We are particularly indebted to him for the appendices and enlarged bibliography, which he has provided for this edition.

We would also gratefully acknowledge the help received from Professor J. W. Dundee, Mr. R. F. R. Gardner, Dr. P. G. R. May, the Rev. H. C. Trowell, and Mr. H. Morgan Williams; and the permission given by Victor Gollancz Ltd. to quote from *Faith Healing* by Dr. Louis Rose (1968).

VINCENT EDMUNDS
C. GORDON SCORER

BIBLICAL REFERENCES

Quotations from the Bible have been taken—except where otherwise stated—from the New International Version (published first in Great Britain in 1979).

CHAPTER I

THE BASIS FOR AN ENQUIRY

During recent years interest in what is known as 'faith-healing' has much increased. In this situation various forms of 'fringe-medicine' have also become more popular. There is more than one reason for this. One is the growing complexity, and with it the greater impersonalism, of the medical services. Another is that Western Medicine as a whole—in spite of its spectacular triumphs in certain directions—has made surprisingly little headway against some of the more common disabling diseases. There has further been the contemporary rise of the various 'Charismatic Movements'* within the Christian Churches which have reported numerous cases of miraculous healing. Similar claims have been made by Spiritualist and other movements. It is probable that—since the Middle Ages—interest in this subject has seldom been higher both in the Church and amongst members of the public than it is today.

'Healing'

It has become, therefore, a duty for all concerned to examine the relevant evidence and accumulated experience concerning this important subject of healing. This has become more difficult, however, because of the present ambiguity in the use of terms. In most cases it is *physical* healing which is meant. But today the word may be extended to cover restoration from mental conditions and the mending of broken relationships (as, for example, in a marriage). It may also be applied to the ending of factions within a community and similar recoveries of unity.

Our English noun 'healing' derives from the Anglo-Saxon adjective *hāl*, which originally described, for example, a warrior who had returned from battle 'whole', 'safe' or 'sound'. Later,

---

* The name arises from the New Testament Greek *charismata* (the plural form of *charisma*—a 'gift'). The adjective 'charismatic' is here used to describe what is claimed to be the restoration of the more spectacular of those spiritual 'gifts', which are described in St. Paul's Epistles as present in the early Church.

in Middle English this term was still being applied to the physical body in the sense of being 'whole' or 'sound'. 'Healing' was, therefore, to restore soundness to the body. In modern English, however, there has been a widening in usage and there is not a completely satisfactory definition of 'health', except in so far as it indicates a general feeling of physical fitness, in which all the faculties are smoothly and silently fulfilling their functions. W. A. R. Thomson's *Concise Medical Dictionary* (Churchill-Livingstone) offers the following definition—'The state of being free from disease mentally and physically; and the body functioning in all respects of its optimum level of efficiency'. An active healthy person is scarcely aware of his body. In the pages which follow the interest will be centred on healing of the *physical* body.

Faith

The word 'faith' comes from the Middle English *'feith'*, itself derived (through Mediaeval French) from *'fidem'*, the accusative case of Latin *'fides'*. It conveys the thought of complete 'confidence' in, or 'reliance' upon, someone or something. Hence, when used in the combination 'faith-healing', it is intended to convey the meaning of a complete (not necessarily dramatic) change in someone who has been seriously ill, but who—instead of resorting to the usual medical means—has regained health by placing his confidence in some person, or agency, possessing healing 'powers'. In this context the emphasis is upon the particular person, or agency, involved in contrast from the 'natural' healing, which occurs spontaneously in many illnesses—with or without medical aid.

In this study the term 'faith healing' has been preferred to other descriptions—such as 'miraculous', 'spiritual', 'divine' or 'mind' healing. Each of the latter adjectives has the disadvantage —which is also shared to a lesser extent by 'faith'—that the causative element in the changed condition is pre-empted. Strictly speaking, all true 'healing' is 'divine'. But by retaining the commoner term 'faith' it is intended to leave the field of reference more open.

Miracle

A discussion of 'miracles' and the miraculous, in general, belongs to the specialised field of Christian Apologetics. It has been ably treated in numerous books by first-class scholars.* The word 'miracle', however, needs to be defined for our present purposes, for it has suffered a good deal of distortion by its over-employment in current usage. Anything at all out of the ordinary, any striking new discovery and any specially good technical invention are each apt to be greeted as a 'miracle'. A medical practitioner, for example, may sometimes jocularly describe an unexpectedly quick recovery, or marked change in a chronic condition, as 'a miracle'. In the majority of cases no one is seriously misled. Sometimes, however, they *are*. Cases have been known where a patient—earlier needing some kind of support—has walked unaided into a surgeon's consulting room and the latter has exclaimed with emphasis 'It is a *miracle!*' It *may*, of course, truly have been a miracle. But the patient's friends received the impression that the surgeon had definitely asserted that it *was* one. The word 'miracle' is surely being overused in contemporary speech to explain the effect that a particular event has had on an observer or to impress a person to whom something pleasant has happened.

The Shorter Oxford English Dictionary defines 'miracle' as follows: 'A marvellous event exceeding the known powers of nature and therefore supposed to be due to the special intervention of the Deity or of some supernatural agency; chiefly an act (e.g. of healing) exhibiting control over the laws of nature, and serving as evidence that the agent is either divine or specially favoured by God'.

In discussing the question of unexpected or possibly miraculous healing in a medical setting, there is a need to keep to recognised definitions which are in agreement with the terminology of Science and Medicine. The more that we know about the resources for repair after injury possessed by the human body the more it becomes a matter for greater wonder. The immediate combination of 'mechanisms' and chemical changes required to effect a repair is baffling in its complexity. Yet we refer to it as a 'natural' event! The word miracle, however—we suggest—should be confined to a rare and wholly inexplicable event. It

* *Miracles, Yesterday and To-day: Real and Counterfeit* (first published under the title '*Counterfeit Miracles 1918*'), B. B. Warfield 1965. Eerdmans, Grand Rapids; *Miracles*, Ed. C. F. D. Moule, 1965, Mowbray; *Miracles*, C. S. Lewis 1947, Geoffrey Bles. There is also a more general discussion: *Healing Miracles*, M. A. H. Melinsky, 1968, Mowbray.

should indicate an occurrence outside the course of ordinary human experience and not simply be applied to something which is uncommon.

Some General Considerations

It is important to recognise that the Christian Church has no monopoly of the concept of 'faith healing'—at least if we use 'faith' in its broadest sense. Other religions and pseudo-religions and cults, together with what are known as 'mind-healing' movements, make similar claims. The following are therefore offered as guidelines to keep the discussion in perspective.*

1. What are termed 'natural'—and, in their own sphere 'psychotherapeutic'—phenomena should as far as possible be kept distinct in our thinking from those cases in which *prima facie* claims are made for *faith* healing. A patient may, for instance, attribute the cure of a simple condition to a particular person or agency, when it would seem to medical observers that his illness took a normal course and his recovery was spontaneous or 'natural'.

2. It follows from this that when the term 'miraculous' is used it is (in this study) confined to cases of demonstrable *'organic'* disease—that is, disease of various organs where the disorder can be seen, shown on an X-ray plate, or a section of the diseased tissue can be examined. In the case of disorders of function (especially those associated with pain), where no organic disease can be shown to exist (and in disorders in the sphere of psychological medicine), it is for obvious reasons much more difficult to be sure of the sequence of events, the reality of the results and their permanence. Conversely when clearly observable *organic* conditions are present, it is easier to attain some basis of comparison between the usual result of medical treatment and instances where there is a claim that there has been 'faith healing'.† [Functional and psychiatric disorders, of course, come equally within the operation of the miraculous, but symptoms are largely what the patient feels, or thinks he feels or cannot do. They are subjective symptoms and, therefore, much more difficult to assess.]

3. There needs also to be agreement concerning a valid definition

---

* The authors are indebted to the Rev. D. Martyn Lloyd-Jones, M.D., M.R.C.P., for permission to adapt one of his characteristically helpful classifications from an informal talk which he gave to a (London) Medical Study Group.

† A later section, pages 57-59 and 86 foot, 87, will refer to the mental aspects of healing.

of 'miracle'—if a case is to be accepted as a true example of 'faith-healing'. Those who accept the authority of the Bible, would take the view that the characteristic features of our Lord's miracles, as recorded in the Gospels, provide us with the most relevant and satisfying criteria for such a purpose.*

4. At the present time two particular claims are being made in Christian circles. First, that the special gifts (*'charismata'*), as they are described in the Pauline Epistles, have once again been restored in our age both to churches and to some individuals. Second, that collectively at its foundation the Church was, and still is, 'divinely commissioned' to heal in this way. It is, therefore, necessary to be clear about what those special gifts actually were and how they were related to the healing miracles of the Lord and those He commissioned to heal. Also, it is important to examine the evidence for expecting that the Church would continue this healing ministry.

5. It is further desirable—though in the nature of the case much more difficult to achieve—that there should be accuracy in assessing the nature of the 'healings', which are found reported by Church Fathers in the first centuries of Church History and, later, during the great spiritual revivals of modern times.

6. In addition, accuracy is needed in assessing factually, scientifically and medically the considerable claims of a large number of contemporary individuals and movements which claim to heal by 'spiritual' or other non-medical means.

7. Finally, in view of their variety, when examining the claims of contemporary movements of healing it is relevant to discriminate concerning the sources in the background to which, or to whom, the healing 'powers' are attributed. 'Faith' may be placed in more than one type, source or token of aid. It may be a specially gifted person, a Spiritualist medium, a particular religious community, a holy relic or some other similar object. The National Federation of Spiritual Healers, which in 1965 claimed nearly 5,000 members, is mainly connected with the Spiritualist churches. Several of the well-known individual 'Healers' were, or are, Spiritualists. They themselves have attributed the efficacy of their work to their various 'mediums' or 'controls'. For example, the late Harry Edwards of the Sanctuary, Shere, Surrey attributed his powers to 'spirit-controls'. At first this was

* See page 63.

a Red Indian, but later it was Pasteur and Lister. In describing the Chapel at the Sanctuary, Beverley Nichols mentions that 'On the walls hang three pictures—one of Jesus and two "spirit portraits" of Pasteur and Lister'.*

Relevant 'Spiritual' Tests

From a Christian point of view, therefore, the question arises: How may a sincere observer distinguish between the various types of 'healing'? How may the claims of some Christian leaders be distinguished from those which are a result of (i) personality and natural gifts; (ii) various forms of suggestion; (iii) hypnotic influence and mesmerism; (iv) the 'spirits' of the departed, acting as mediums, or, possibly (v) witchcraft and evil forces? Christian observers have usually approached the problem along such lines as the following:

1. In the cases of miraculous healing reported in the Bible, there is ordinarily a marked absence of any symbol which is unnecessarily strange or wonder-provoking. They are unaccompanied by an unusual vision, or the production of a revered object such as (to cite from mediaeval examples) a bone of an early martyr saint or a button from a garment of the Virgin Mary.

2. In later Church History there is usually evidence of earnest prayer on the part of a church, of a near relative, or of some devout fellow-Christian.

3. The person who is responsible for, or 'performing', the miracles does not court popularity, but tends to be well in the background. Here we must certainly contrast unfavourably the showmanship of some present-day healers (even in Christian circles) with our Lord's 'tell no man', or the anxiety of the Apostles in the reports in the Acts not to take any credit to themselves. There are, it is true, in some of the contemporary movements 'reluctant healers' from natural modesty or shyness. But, in some modern examples, 'showmanship' appears to be more in evidence than one could wish.

4. In the New Testament cases it appears that a special commission from God had been given. Those concerned seemed to know in their hearts that a miracle of healing was about to happen. All the power is regarded as retained in the

* 'Harry Edwards: Thirty Years a Spiritual Healer' (Herbert Jenkins: London 1968) page 69. A footnote adds: 'These have since been removed'.

hands of God. His servants remain simply channels speaking with conviction and with authority in His Name. A clear statement and demonstration of this fact was given by Peter at the Temple gate* and by Paul at Lystra.†

5. A miracle in the New Testament context was always followed by the presence of awe, fear and the worship of God. The typical response on the part of both those who were the instruments of healing and those who were healed, was to give praise to God.

Experience suggests that it is by applying the five tests mentioned above that it may be possible to differentiate between a healing which is the result of a man's strong personality and natural 'powers', and one which is a true intervention by God and apart from human means.

Such considerations prompt a crucial question in a Christian context: Has God endowed the church with a special gift of healing? Should it be our normal experience to see cures being regularly effected today by such divine supernatural forces and without other means? As B. B. Warfield has put it,‡ does the Bible's account of faith 'give us as clear a title to the healing of our bodies as to the salvation of our souls?' There have been, and are, those who claim that it does. Others would interpret the biblical statements somewhat differently.

The Limitations of Medical Opinion

On several occasions Dr. Martyn Lloyd-Jones has called the attention of various study groups to a common misconception in studies of this kind. He has emphasised that it is too readily assumed that a scientist or a doctor—who is also a Christian—has some unique advantage or authority in determining whether a given phenomenon is, or is not, a divine miracle. It must always be kept in mind that scientifically and medically trained persons (however Christian) are subject to the same intellectual limitations and powers of observation as any other observers of equal ability in other walks of life. The most that scientific and medical training can do (in this context) is to assist in determining the extent to which a given phenomenon must be regarded as *exceptional in clinical medical experience.*

* Acts 3:1-11. † Acts 14:8-11.
‡ *Miracles: Yesterday and To-day.* B. B. Warfield. 1965.

The Method of Approach

In what follows the authors have approached by examining the viewpoints expressed concerning this subject during Church History. These have then been compared with the reports of contemporary cases of 'faith healing'. Primarily the available literature has been surveyed with particular attention to the teaching of the Bible. The views of various medical practitioners, who have worked in this area, have been sought. Finally attempts have been made to obtain a series of well documented cases which would substantiate these claims and permit a sufficiently satisfying comparison. Although there has been a good deal of work and much correspondence, the results (both in range and documentation of the findings from contemporary experience) have been considerably less than had been expected. It is clearly a subject which invites continued study.

Chapter II

THE GENERAL EVIDENCE OF THE BIBLE

We tend to take it for granted that the Bible will present us with a clearly definitive statement on such matters as this, which will leave no doubt about what the original writers intended to convey. Indeed, healing miracles are *factually* described in both the Old and New Testaments. However, interpreting the records of the miracles in their contexts, in order to decide the nature of their purpose, has led to a variety of opinions amongst biblical scholars. For example, in the case of the New Testament there is a major divergence of view between (i) those who believe that miracles similar to those which are presented in the Gospels (and the Acts of the Apostles) were intended to continue on into the second and subsequent centuries of Church History; and (ii) those who believe that the type of miracle performed by the Lord and His Apostles had a distinctive relevance, and were unique, to the Apostolic age. In this view the miracles were destined to cease with the last of the Apostles and those whom they had commissioned. A brief summary will be given of the main biblical references to healing.

1. *The Old Testament*

On a number of occasions in the Old Testament there are reports that God miraculously acted to cause events for which there is no natural, or 'scientific', explanation for what happened and which were quite outside ordinary human experience. Yet, in view of the many centuries covering the whole of Israel's long history, the number of such miracles seems to be comparatively small—at least, they are fewer than we might have expected. Several aspects in the descriptions and timing of these events, however, would appear to throw some light on their purpose.

First, there is the significant fact that these events are not distributed evenly throughout the Old Testament books. The miracles are grouped around two eras of crisis in the story of

Israel. The first group* comes in the chain of events leading up to Israel's deliverance from Egypt, their 40 years of wandering in the Wilderness and their final occupation of the land promised to them. The second group† is found during the life-times of the two prophets Elijah and Elisha. This was a period at which Israel's fortunes were at their lowest during the oppressive tyranny of Ahab and Jezebel. In both epochs God acted decisively on behalf of Israel and spoke authoritatively to the nation and to their oppressors. Relative to the total record, the more *spectacular* miracles are found at these points of dramatic national deliverance.

There are three main views, which are largely complementary, concerning the concept of miracle in the Old Testament. F. C. Lindars‡ summarises these as (i) that a miracle is regarded as a personal act of God; (ii) that, however, God frequently uses a human agent in performing His unusual acts; and (iii) that, sometimes, the miracles are attributed to the human agent himself in a way which seems intended to underline the holiness, or special faithfulness, of that particular servant of God.

The Old Testament general references to health conveys the impression that, in the minds of the writers, all health is in the hand of God. The devout Hebrew trusted in a personal God and believed that His providence covered all forms of his well being, including health. One of the revelations, which accompanied the Covenant with Israel, was God's declaration 'I am the Lord who heals you'. § Again, David in Psalm 103, when calling upon his soul to bless the Lord, adds significantly 'He forgives all my sins and heals all my diseases'. It is also noteworthy that there is a reference in Deuteronomy‖ to what might be called a 'prophylactic miracle'. The people of Israel were promised by God that, if they would obey Him, 'The Lord will keep you free from every disease. He will not inflict on you the horrible diseases you knew in Egypt, but He will inflict them all those who hate you.'

* The Books of Exodus and Joshua.

† The Books of I and II Kings.

‡ F. C. Lindars 'Elijah, Elisha and the Gospel Miracles' in *Miracles*. Ed. C. E. Moule 1965. Mowbrays.

§ Exodus 15:26.

‖ Deuteronomy 7:15.

2. *The New Testament*

In the New Testament—as in the case of the Old—the reported miracles are again grouped into two main periods. The first group takes place in the early part of our Lord's three years of ministry, and the second group occurs during the first phase of the growth of the Church, following Pentecost. Outside of the Gospels and the Acts, there is very little further reference to healing miracles. The Epistle of James, which is regarded as one of the earliest of the apostolic letters, makes a single well-known reference to the subject. Apart, however, from the general mention in the lists of the gifts in I Corinthians to 'gifts of healings' (a double plural), the rest of the New Testament is silent on this matter. It is for this reason that Biblical scholars, who follow the traditional Protestant interpretation, suggest that the interest of the New Testament writers in recording miracles of healing appears to be concentrated on their value for two purposes:

(i) To confirm the message of John the Baptist* (and His own claims) that Christ was indeed Israel's Messiah, appointed to be her Prophet, Priest and King; and as a sign that the Kingdom of God was now present amongst the people of Israel. The Servant of God was to be One who would 'take up our infirmities and carry our sorrows'.

(ii) To confirm the fact that the Apostles were the accredited heralds of the New Covenant and the foundation stones in Christ's Church.† The fact that the miracles of the Apostles were similar to those wrought by the Messiah, underlined their authority at the outset of their leadership of the new People of God.

Those who take this view would also go on to point out that (if this interpretation be correct) it gives the main clue to God's purpose in impressing the people of Israel by means of miraculous signs, including the miracles of healing.

Classifying the Miracles

There are several ways in which the miracles of healing in the Gospels might be classified. There is a large group of forty-one

* See pages 35, 36.
† See pages 39-41.

cases in which *individuals* are reported as healed;* and, then, there are ten reports of the healing of *crowds* of sick people. The multitudes crowded to Him and he had 'compassion' on them.† In the records of these cases it is important to observe the sweepingly inclusive nature of the descriptions given. Christ is said to have 'healed every disease and sickness among the people', 'all who touched Him were healed' and He 'healed all who were under the power of the devil'. Not only 'every disease and sickness' were said to be healed but the people came in from 'throughout the whole region'. In other words, not only were some forty-one individuals cured (and the details are provided), but whole communities were healed of many forms of disease and disability prevalent in Israel at the time.

Other classifications have emphasised the different types of the diseases cured. In this case the observer cannot fail to be impressed by the wide range of types of disease which were cured. For, in spite of all the recent advances in Medicine, and its increasing number of technical specialities, the conditions described could not today easily be corrected by Western Medicine. Certainly it could not be done—to use one of Mark's favourite words—'immediately'. Also in the list of individual cases there are examples which would need to be treated in several specialised departments of a modern hospital. For example, there are (at least) five cases of paralysis, five of blindness and eleven of leprosy—not to speak of the cases of menorrhagia, scoliosis, fever, deafness, mutism, oedema and epilepsy. To match the restoration of Malchus' severed ear would today call for immediate action in favourable conditions and speedy admission to a plastic surgery unit.

Delegation to the Disciples

In addition to the references to Christ's own healing miracles, the Gospels also report two occasions when first the Apostles and then seventy 'other disciples' were sent out by Christ on preaching missions, during which they were given the power to heal. Early in the Gospels, we read that the Lord gave 'authority' to the Apostles‡ 'to drive out evil spirits, and to cure every kind of

* *Healing and Christianity.* Morton T. Kelsey. 1973. S.C.M. Press.
† See Appendix I. for a list of the main references.
‡ Matt. 10:1.

disease and sickness'.   Later, 'seventy others' (some of the early MSS say 'seventy-two') were commissioned to serve as advance parties* going ahead ('two by two') into the towns and villages into which He Himself would later be coming.   In other words, they would demonstrate by sample healings what He would do to the many when He came.†

Similar 'group' healings, performed through Apostles and evangelists, are also reported on ten occasions in the Acts of the Apostles.‡   There are also in the Acts of the Apostles nine incidents of the healing of individuals, ranging from the man 'crippled from birth' lying at the Beautiful gate of the Temple, to Paul's healing of the father of Publius in Malta.§   These cases include—two raised from the dead, one spirit exorcised, two cripples made to walk, the healing of one case of paralysis and another of fever, the restoration of sight, and recovery from snake-bite.   As in the case of the accounts in the Gospels, the reader is given to understand (i) that a wide range of pathological states were cured and (ii) that considerable numbers of people were involved.   Again, the factual reporting in the Acts of the Apostles of cases of raising from the dead and of exorcism suggests that they are to be accepted in the same way as their parallels in the Gospels.

The Remainder of the New Testament

As already commented, apart from the Gospels and the Acts, there is very little further reference to the question of healing in the rest of the New Testament.   If the Charismatic gifts were destined to be of special importance to the later history of the Church it seems strange how little emphasis the apostolic writers seem to place on them.   Peter, John and the writer of the Epistle to the Hebrews all make no mention of them.   Apart from the classic passage of I Corinthians 12-14, Paul himself also gives them little other attention.   The message of the New Testament Epistles is primarily concerned with the contents and spread of the Gospel, associated doctrinal matters, and the practical administration of the Church Community.

† Luke 10:1-17.
† See Appendix III page 97.
‡ Acts 5:12-16; 8:5-8; 14:3; 19:11-12; 28:9.
§ See Appendix III page 97.

In Paul's three lists of the 'spiritual gifts', * he mentions 'gifts of healings' (two plurals)† and this is all in the one epistle, I Corinthians. They are given a bare mention with little explanation about their meaning and use. Also the primary object of the classic Corinthians passage (chapters 12-14) seems to be a discouragement of the misuses by the Corinthians of the gift of speaking in other languages.

The additional important reference to healing in the New Testament is that which mentions prayer for the sick in James 5:13-20. The more, however, this passage is considered *in its context* the more it would seem that any new reader coming to it for the first time, and without any presuppositions, would arrive at only one conclusion. The teaching of the chapter is primarily directed towards the importance and power of prayer and intercession and, in the verse concerned, it is advocating a special form of prayer meeting for a sick person.‡

We would submit that the simple biblical accounts of the healing miracles compel the view that the writers expected their descriptions of cases of healing to be accepted as direct acts of God. For the devout Hebrew in Old Testament times, Israel's divine Lord providentially superintended his personal health. Similarly, to the authors of the New Testament, God was close at hand for His people. His healing acts through Christ and the Apostles (when acting as His deputies) were in keeping with the delegation of 'all authority' to the Lord of the Church.§ The biblical accounts are also free from great 'marvels' introduced (for example in the Apocryphal Gospels) for the sake of making a dramatic display. Each miracle had a purpose in the human situation in which 'the God Who heals' had come near to mankind in our Lord Jesus Christ acting as 'His Servant'. In the Acts, He is similarly brought near to men through the witness of the Apostles, who were His 'Servant's' servants. As the Psalmist had prophesied—'Surely His salvation is near those who fear Him that His glory may dwell in our land. Love and faithfulness meet

* I Cor. 12:8-10; 28-31.

† The possible meaning of the plurals is discussed on page 41.

‡ This is discussed further on pages 42, 43 and see R. V. G. Tasker: *The Epistle of James*. Tyndale Press, New Testament Commentaries.

§ Matt. 28:18-20.

together; righteousness and peace kiss each other.   Faithfulness springs forth from the earth and righteousness looks down from heaven.'*

* Ps. 85:9,10.

Chapter III

TWO VIEWS OF THE CHARISMATA

During the history of New Testament interpretation several viewpoints have been advanced to explain references to what have been known as 'the gifts of grace',* and 'the signs' or 'mark' of an Apostle,† that is, the special powers of those who led the first century Christian congregations. As indicated above, there are two chief contemporary views. These may be conveniently described as the 'traditional Protestant' view which has come down from the time of the Reformation, and that of the various modern 'Pentecostal Movements'. Since the beginning of the twentieth century the essential difference between them is that those who hold to the first believe that the internal evidence of the Bible indicates that the more spectacular gifts were appointed specially for the duration of the Apostolic Age and then, having completed their purpose, were gradually withdrawn. Those who advance the second view are equally convinced that the gifts—as listed in the Epistles‡—were permanently granted to the Church, and that during those periods in history, when they have been little in evidence, it has been because the Church has suffered from their neglect. They would further claim that in recent years there has been a renewal of the more striking of these gifts—such as the three gifts of prophecy, 'tongues' and healing.

It must suffice here to make sufficient reference to Church history to set these two viewpoints into true perspective. The important periods have been (1) the 'Apostolic Age', lasting from the commissioning of the 'Apostles' and 'the Seventy' until the death of the last Apostle; (2) the period of their successors (that is, the two centuries of writing by the Apostolic Fathers, the Ante-Nicene Fathers', Origen and Cyprian—who became Bishop of

---

* Gr. *Charismata* (plural of *Charisma*) 'a gift, freely and graciously bestowed'; 'a favour bestowed'. W. Bauer's Lexicon, trans. W. F. Arndt and F. W. Gringrich.
† II Cor. 12:12.
‡ As in I Cor. 12:8-10 and 28-31; Rom. 12:6-8; Eph. 4:11.

Carthage in 248—until Constantine's edict bringing toleration for the church in 313) and (3) subsequent Church history. The tendency in some schools of thought has been to suggest that one of the chief results of official toleration of the Church introduced by Constantine was a decline from the earlier high standards of spirituality and Christian action. For example, the deterioration is usually dated from the beginning of 'the political establishment of the Church and consequent loss of the earlier triumphant Christian faith'. We must pause to reflect, however, that if God saw fit to grant a period of immunity from persecution in order to allow the Church to grow and at last enjoy a measure of peace and prosperity, one would scarcely expect that all the results would need to be deplored. Spiritual loss and the spread of erroneous views arise from other and more radical causes.

View I: The Traditional View; the Cessation of the Spectacular Gifts.

The German biblical scholar Adolf Schlatter, in an article on the Holy Spirit, writes: 'The sign was an essential element in the equipment of the prophet. This appears from the fact that, in the miraculous narratives of the New Testament, miracles are not represented as everyday events which may occur in the experience of all believers, but are valued as special provision for the work of those who bear a special commission. The Gospels . . . the Book of Acts, and the utterances of St. Paul, regarding his 'signs', all show distinctly that miracles were intimately related to the apostolic function.'

Those holding this view believe that the 'Charismatic era' in the Church lasted from the Resurrection of Christ (or, from Pentecost) until the point at which the Gospel was finally rejected by Israel's leaders, and then was offered more fully to the Gentiles. They regard Acts 28:28 as indicating this turning point. It was the Jews, as St. Paul tells us, who were looking for the 'signs' of Messiah's coming, whereas the Greeks were looking for 'wisdom'. The sign at Pentecost had been in the form of the ability of the Apostles, Galileans, to speak the vernacular languages (in the Greek of Acts 2, the 'mother-tongues') of the pilgrims who had come to Jerusalem for the Feast. It was the clear indication that the kingdom of heaven had now been opened to all believers and was no longer confined to the people of the Old Covenant. The Apostles then went on to perform miracles similar to those of

Messiah and some of the people—including many rabbis—believed, though most of Israel's leaders rejected the Gospel. The point was then reached at which 'the signs' had fulfilled their purpose and ceased.

Of the numerous scholarly studies of the 'Charismata' from this viewpoint, two of the clearest and most usefully documented for our purposes are those (i) by the late B. B. Warfield, Professor of Princeton Theological Seminary, New Jersey (1887-1921) and (ii) by J. S. McEwen, formerly Professor of Church History, Christ's College, Aberdeen. Professor Warfield's book developed from the Thomas Smyth Lectures (1917-18) in the Columbia Theology Seminary, South Carolina. It was originally published under the title of *Counterfeit Miracles* (1918), later republished in paper back as *Miracles: Yesterday and Today, True and False* (1965 Eerdmans, Grand Rapids). J. S. McEwen's study was entitled *The Ministry of Healing* and appeared in the *Scottish Journal of Theology* (1954) 7 p. 133. Both writers are primarily concerned to put the question of the various spiritual gifts into the perspective of the New Testament, before tracing their course in subsequent Church History. They also call attention to the somewhat scanty references made to this subject in the writings of the earliest Fathers. Their chief finding in the patristic writings was that in the first century 'exorcisms' had been prevalent, whereas miraculous healings of the type under present discussion were difficult to find. Warfield—a well informed and accurate worker—does not hesitate to make some strong statements. For example, he claims that the evidence of history is that the special miraculous gifts had virtually ceased with the Apostles. He also declares that not only is there no evidence for them between that age and the fourth century, but that the Ante-Nicene Fathers were much concerned to know *why* they had ceased. They quoted only very rare occurrences of healing. Except for a possible reference by Origen, the Fathers write as if they themselves had not seen any such miracles and none of them claims this gift for himself. They themselves seem to be aware that their lack in this respect was in marked contrast to the contemporary stories of miracles taking place in the heathen shrines around them. It was not until the later days of Augustine (almost A.D. 400) that there are descriptions of miracle-working Christian shrines, and Augustine, as bishop, seems to have begun to promote them. Later—

particularly in the Middle Ages—Roman Catholic Christianity became associated with a series of miracles connected with the saints, relics of the saints, healing shrines, and holy wells. It continued to make such claims, though with less publicity and with more restraint in the detail, after the Renaissance and Protestant Reformation.

On the other hand, Warfield believes that the extent of the presence, degree of diffusion and the effects of the miraculous gifts in the era of the Apostles has been very much underestimated by later Christians. He writes 'We are justified in considering it characteristic of the Apostolic churches that miraculous gifts should be displayed in them. The exception would be, not a Church with, but a Church without, such gifts. Everywhere, the Apostolic Church was marked out as itself a gift from God, by showing forth the possession of the Spirit in appropriate works of the Spirit, miracles of healing, miracles of power, and miracles of knowledge, whether in the form of prophecy, discerning of Spirits, miracles of speech, whether in the gift of tongues or their interpretation. The Apostolic Church was a miracle-working church.' He is emphatic about the widespread influence of this state of affairs in New Testament times. He also has a number of valuable comments on the nature of the gifts themselves.*

He further emphasises that St. Paul is concerned that the 'higher gifts'—faith, hope and love—should lead the Church in 'a still more excellent way'. Similarly, amongst the more spectacular gifts themselves it is 'prophecy' that is singled out by the Apostle Paul for special emphasis. This gift is described as the power of bringing uplifting teaching and exhortation in order that the body of Christ should be 'edified'.

At the opening of his study, Professor J. S. M. McEwen makes the significant remark 'It is a common delusion of the Christian mind that the Church in the past possessed all the virtues that the Church in the present manifestly lacks. Secular man justifies his civilisation by dreaming of its ideal future. Christian man justifies his Church by dreaming of its ideal past. And there is probably a good deal of fantasy in both ideals.' He then goes on to take a searching look at the documentation.

He notes that 'modern advocates of spiritual healing have, in general, shown more enthusiasm than critical acumen in their

* *Miracles: Yesterday and To-day.* Pages 3-6 and Chapter II pp. 25ff.

handling of the evidence they have drawn from the writings of the
Early Fathers'. He scrutinizes the usual quotations from the
writings of Justin Martyr, Tertullian, Irenaeus and Origen. He
finds little to show that they possessed, or used, any miraculous
powers in the healing of disease. The Fathers speak *often* of
exorcism of evil spirits, but they are distinctly reticent concerning
miracles of healing, or raising from the dead. McEwen's inference
from these writings is that the healings had taken place some time
in the past, and, for example, neither Irenaeus nor Origen, who
alone really report them as contemporary phenomena claim
(with the possible exception of the latter) to have been eye-
witnesses.

The first three centuries are of particular importance, for as
McEwen says 'By the fourth century we are well into the era of the
miraculous cures wrought by holy relics and martyrs'. Evidence
at this stage becomes confused and reported miracles are exaggerated and the descriptions are sometimes quite fantastic. He
suggests that such pretentious claims may well have been borrowed
from the pagan cults and were proof of the growing worldliness of
the Church. Such marvels continued to be part of the Church's
'witness' up till the time of the Reformation.

In summary, both B. B. Warfield and J. S. M. McEwen believe
that the writings of the Apostles as preserved in the New Testament, give no grounds for the belief that the later Church was
intended permanently to possess special powers of 'languages' or
physical healing. Apart from a single reference in I Peter 4:10, it
is only Paul who refers to the 'gifts of grace' or 'spiritual gifts'. It
is noteworthy that he himself goes out of the way to emphasise the
importance of those gifts which were not spectacular, and to
recommend that the Corinthians should pursue *these*, rather than
those which—in current exaggerated forms—he tells them to put
in their due place. He himself was not healed of his 'thorn in the
flesh' and recommends a means of medication for Timothy's
gastritis. John and Peter make no reference to healing of the
body. James, in what is believed to be one of the earliest written
epistles, makes one important reference in the context of prayer.
In their view of the available evidence, therefore, neither B. B.
Warfield nor J. S. McEwen believe that the first three centuries
substantiate the claim that the 'healing gifts' (undoubtedly
possessed by the Apostles, or some of them) were lost through the

neglect and unfaithfulness of the Church. The special gifts had fulfilled their primary purpose and ceased.

View II. The Perpetuation of the Charismatic Gifts.

Historically, in nineteenth century England at least, the renewed theological interest in the special gifts of grace began around the years 1828-1832 through an eloquent and popular preacher, Edward Irving, who was at that time Minister of Regent Square Presbyterian Church, London.*

Earlier, on certain occasions during the periods of great spiritual revivals, there had been what *prima facie* would seem to have been well-authenticated reports of healings, and which the local Church leaders regarded as supernatural. For example, associated with John Wesley's remarkable evangelistic tours in the second half of the eighteenth century were phenomena which contemporary observers regarded as supernatural. These are not to be lightly dismissed as cases of mass 'hysteria'. It is interesting that the majority of these incidents took place in the earlier years of his preaching, though a few occurred at intervals later. One of the best informed of Wesley's early biographers —L. Tyerman—provides a list of such happenings during the period of his preaching to the Religious Societies.†

Cases of faith healing were not a prominent feature of the Eighteenth Century Revival. Wesley is introduced here because on several occasions he gave his views on the continuity of the Charismatic gifts. Throughout his life—sometimes at the cost of apparent inconsistency—Wesley indicates that he would rather be considered superstitious or even heretical, than fail to recognise a true work of God when it was occurring. Referring to the tremblings and other phenomena accompanying the preaching he says 'These circumstances are common at the dawn of a work, but afterwards uncommon'. Alluding to the early Church movements such as that of the Montanists, he suggests 'the grand reason why the miraculous gifts were so soon withdrawn, was, not only that faith and holiness were well-nigh lost, but that dry, formal, orthodox men began even to ridicule whatever gifts they had not themselves; and to deny them all, as either madness or

---

* A fuller reference to Irving is made on pages 52, 53.

† L. Tyerman's *Life and Times of John Wesley.* (3 Vols.) 1876. Vol. 1, 255-268.

imposture'. Finally, in his preface to the first volume of Sermons, he states 'There is nothing either in the Old Testament or the New which teaches that miracles were to be confined within the limits of the apostolic or the Cyprianic age, or, that God hath in any way precluded Himself from working miracles in any kind or degree, in any age to the end of time'. After an occasion where Whitfield had protested to Wesley about the dramatic effects of some of the latter's sermons and, then, the next day had had four hearers fall to the ground during his own next sermon, Wesley makes the following entry in his diary (7th July, 1739) 'From this time, I trust we shall all suffer God to carry on His own work in the way that pleaseth Him'.(!) Whilst in those times less allowance was made for the physical effects of strong emotion, the nationwide reality of spiritual revival in the 18th century is a fact of history.

To return to the Nineteenth Century. About 1828 Edward Irving began to be interested in certain reported cases of miraculous healing, and, what he believed to be, a rebirth of 'the gifts of grace', in the Lowlands of Scotland. A little later in his own London church, some of the members of his congregation gave signs of possessing what he welcomed as the gifts of 'prophecy' and of 'tongues'. Space precludes a detailed discussion here of the debates at the time and the founding of the 'Catholic Apostolic Church' with its special emphasis upon the renewed 'Charismata'. Irving is important because his Church has been regarded by historians as the original source in Britain of such nineteenth century interest as there was in this subject.

It was not, however, until the beginning of the twentieth century that there came from America, in 1907 and 1908, the first representatives of the Pentecostal Movement. Their views then attracted wide attention. This movement strongly claimed that the special gifts of grace *should* have been in full operation amongst Christian people down the centuries, but had fallen into disuse because the Church of Christ had been unfaithful. Because of the special healing meetings run throughout the country by the Pentecostal Movement, more notice of these views was taken in the main Churches and the issue became studied by some of their leaders. For example, a study was produced in 1909 by Canon Percy Dearmer (at that time Vicar of Hampstead and, later, Canon of Westminster Abbey) entitled 'Body and Soul'. It was not, however, until after the immense suffering during the

1914-1918 First World War that (in Britain at least) much greater general interest began to be apparent.

In more recent times, perhaps the most influential book produced in theological circles was a London University thesis published by Evelyn Frost in 1940, entitled *Christian Healing*, with the subtitle: 'A Consideration of the Place of Spiritual Healing in the Church of Today in the Light of the Doctrine and Practice of the Ante-Nicene Church'. In this book the author has sought to examine the evidence from the Patristic literature over the first three-hundred years of Church History. She has reproduced quotations from the Ante-Nicene Fathers which had been little studied from this point of view by the earlier Patristic scholars, who had mainly been concerned with the history of doctrine. The thesis finally claims that it can be established that during these earlier centuries the Church was engaged in a healing mission and that the more spectacular 'gifts of grace' were in operation throughout these times. Though the subject of her book is primarily concerned with the (physical) healing of disease, the author goes on to state that 'the radical principle underlying it can be equally applied to healing of all kinds—physical, mental, spiritual, individual, social and international'.

The foreword claims that it is attention to 'the teaching of the Early Church, as well as copying her example, that will lead the Church of today back to the fuller practice of Divine Healing, through the sacrament of Divine Unction, and the laying on of hands, and the corporate intercession of her members'. In the final words of the preface, 'It is hoped that, by recapturing once more the vision of her infallible power and her definite vocation to bring healing and fuller life to the body, mind and spirit of individuals and to the world so torn ... the Christian Church may effectively save men and nations in the hour of their need, and thus fulfil her true destiny as the extension of the Incarnation of the Saviour of the world'.

Of the subsequent interest in these aspects of the subject, perhaps the best books for the purpose of following up Dr. Evelyn Frost's pioneer study are: L. D. Weatherhead (1951) *Psychology, Religion and Healing* and (edited by) J. Crowlesmith (1962) *Religion and Medicine*. The latter was produced by the (former)Methodist Society for Medical and Pastoral Psychology and is regarded by many as still one of the most useful studies of its kind.

A new body of literature has arisen in the last ten years chiefly out of the 'Charismatic Movement' which has come to have a widespread influence throughout the world—including the Roman Catholic Church.   Selection is difficult, but amongst the best—for careful consideration of the biblical and patristic data— are (i) *The Healing Ministry of the Church* by Bernard Martin (Minister, Geneva) 1960;* (ii) the comprehensive study by a leading authority on healing in the Roman Catholic Church— Francis MacNutt, entitled *Healing* (1974)† and (iii) an equally wide ranging study by Morton T. Kelsey, Assistant Professor in the graduate Department of Education, University of Notre Dame, Indiana—*Healing and Christianity: In Ancient Thought and Modern Times* (1973).‡

The last twelve years has also seen an increase in the number of studies directed to the Church and the community aspect of the 'healing ministry'.   Typical amongst these are *The Healing Church* (1965), by the World Council of Churches; *Community, Church and Healing*, R. A. Lambourne (1963) and *The Church is Healing*, M. Wilson (1966).   There is also a growing more popular literature, in smaller and cheaper form, produced by the Charismatic Movement, of which *Reflected Glory*, A. Smail (1975), *As at the Beginning*, Michael Harper (1965) and *Healing Adventure*, Anne White (1971) have been regarded as the most representative.

In their various ways all of these sources agree on certain propositions concerning the nature, scope and continuity, of the 'gifts of grace'.   They claim that the Church of Jesus Christ has a responsibility for 'the whole man', that is, the bodies as well as the souls of its members on the grounds that 'in addition to the commission of evangelizing the world, the Lord entrusted the Church with a particular ministry in relation to the sick'.   As put by Dr. Michael Wilson this view is that: 'Jesus's works of healing were a normal part of His daily work. . . .   There was in His work no separation of preaching and healing; His words healed, and His healing works loudly proclaimed the rule and purposes of God. . . .   Just as Jesus worked with sick people in many different ways according to their need, so the Church today meets men's needs in various ways.   In the Acts and the Epistles we see the

---

* Lutterworth Press, London.
† Ave Maria Press, Notre Dame, Indiana.
‡ S.C.M. Press, London.

development of Jesus' work by a community—the Church. . . . If we are faithful to this task, there will be associated with it the work of healing the sick.   The unit of the Church's healing work is the local congregation.'*

Another way of stating the case will be found in the first fifty pages of Francis MacNutt's book where he argues from his own and contemporary experience back to our Lord's works of healing. He claims that the Greek implies 'acts of power', rather than 'miracles' (that is, to inspire wonder).   Then, having shown that our Lord delegated first to the Apostles, and, then the Seventy, ability to perform His acts of power—at least for the particular missions entrusted to them—the author continues 'the early Church, the early Christians, had the same power to preach, to heal and to cast out demons that Jesus had.   The Church is the continuation of Jesus' saving power in history.'   (It is to be noted that it is really at this point, i.e. the claim that His disciples had 'the *same* power . . . that Jesus had' that the two schools of thought really diverge.)

Since in the Acts of the Apostles it was not only *Apostles* who were able to heal, but Philip the Evangelist, Stephen and Ananias, the further inference is made that 'The clear implication is that healing and liberation are part of the mission of the Church'. This second claim also represents an important point of divergence between the two main historic viewpoints.   It is best illustrated (on p. 56 of MacNutt's book) by the interpretation given of Acts 4:29-30, where the persecuted infant Church prays 'help your servants to proclaim your message with boldness, by stretching out your hand to heal and to work miracles and marvels through your Name'.   MacNutt comments: 'Notice that they did not pray to preach *and* to heal, but to preach *by* healing.   They preached the message of salvation by actually continuing the work of Jesus.   A doctrine of God's salvation without salvation actually taking place, or a concept of healing—without healing taking place—is empty rhetoric.   Perhaps this is why so much of today's preaching impresses people as abstract and irrelevant.'

Two other important points made by those who share this second alternative viewpoint are that (i) there is no statement in the New Testament that the commission 'to preach and heal' was withdrawn from the Church; and (ii) our Lord in His teaching

* M. Wilson: *The Church is Healing.*   (1966.)

implies that His followers can continue His work in most of its aspects. Again to quote MacNutt 'There is no indication that at sometime the Charismatic dimension of the Church will cease or that its main purpose is to build up the institution to such a point that the structured elements can carry on under their own power'. Then, taking the Lord's words in John 14:12, he would apply them to all aspects of His works, which are suitable to human agents. The Lord said 'I tell you most solemnly, whoever believes in Me will perform the same works I do myself; he will perform even greater works, because I am going to the Father'.

Three Key Verses for the Charismatic Movement

Those who take the view outlined above by Francis MacNutt interpret the verse he quotes last (John 14:12) to imply that an ordinary Church member—'anyone who has faith in Me'—has a clear commission from God to heal the sick. Similarly the phrase which follows 'He will do even greater things than these' is taken to mean that he will do greater *miracles*. But, we must ask, is this our Lord's meaning? Does it not, in the context, rather imply that the resurrection and ascension (His 'going to the Father') will mean the giving of the Holy Spirit, with the spiritual results recorded in the Acts of the Apostles as, for example, Peter's sermon on the day of Pentecost?

B. F. Westcott in his Commentary on John's Gospel interprets the word 'greater' as 'including the wider spiritual effects of their preaching which followed after Pentecost. There is no reference to miracles of a more extraordinary kind, as if there is a possibility of this material comparison. Nor can "greater" be regarded as equivalent to "more". These "greater works" are also *works of Christ* being done by those who "believe in Him".'

Then, again, the Great Commission—in the form given in Mark 16:15-18—is regarded as authorising the view that the more spectacular gifts will continue to accompany the Gospel into the later history of the Church. Whilst Matthew's form of the Great Commission* mentions only the duty to 'make disciples, to baptise and to teach them to obey' Christ's Commandment, Mark's version contains the fuller details—'These signs will accompany those who believe: In My name they will drive out demons; they will speak in new tongues; they will pick up snakes

* Matt. 28:18-20

with their hands, and when they drink deadly poison, it will not hurt them at all; they will place their hands on sick people, and they will get well'.

There is a very real textual problem here. For, whilst in general much of the (subjective) criticism of modern scholars in handling the text of the Bible must be viewed with reserve, there is in this case considerable documentary evidence that Mark's Gospel (as it has come down to us) ends at verse 8. At this point the Modern Versions (the Revised Standard Version, the New English Bible and the New International Version) have had to reckon with the fact that—in the words of the N.I.V.—'The most reliable early Manuscripts do not have Mark 16:9-20'. It seems that either the original ending of Mark was at verse 8, or the original last section of the Gospel was lost during times of persecution and this section added from another source. The New Testament scholar W. J. Conybeare found written against the last part of the chapter in a 10th Century Armenian manuscript in the patriarchal library at Edschmiatzin 'Of the presbyter Ariston'. The remaining verses followed this. The suggestion seemed to be that Ariston added them himself, or found them in another MS. and appended them. It would seem that it would be wiser to rely upon Matthew's version of the Great Commission.

In the more popular, and less scholarly, literature of the Charismatic Movement, the suggestion is sometimes made that because phrases in Isaiah 53:4, 5 are linked to Matthew 8:17, it is therefore implied that our Lord's atonement not only made spiritual reconciliation, but also *atoned* for our sicknesses. But, first, this application is made to the life of our Lord prior to His act of atonement. Also, in Matthew the reference in the context is to the driving away of spirits from many of those who were demon-possessed and also healing of the sick, and Matthew has added 'This was to fulfil what was spoken through the prophet Isaiah: "He took up our infirmities and carried our diseases".' This quotation from the Old Testament has led some Charismatic writers to speak of a 'dual redemption'. It must be said that this is scarcely in keeping with the rest of the Bible, except that at the consummation of the age, that is, at our Lord's Coming, 'the lowly bodies' of Christians will 'put on immortality'!

Those of the traditional view, who regard the primary purpose of the healing miracles as the authentication of our Lord's

Messiahship, would take this reference in Matthew as an important corroboration for their opposite interpretation! With it they would compare Christ's reply to John's messengers in Matthew 11:1-6 (see page 36).

Summary

The reader will see from the above that the main reasons for the divergence of opinion arise from differences in interpretation at three main points—(i) the nature and purpose of the supernatural happenings during the life of our Lord; (ii) the nature and purpose of the powers delegated to the Apostles, and (iii) the intended durability of these special powers in the Early Church—that is, whether they were intended to continue throughout the history of the Church.

The difference can only be resolved (and the reader enabled to make up his own mind) on the basis of (i) an accurate exegesis and interpretation in their context of the Bible's statements; and (ii) a review of the later historical evidence concerning the experience of the Church. In the next chapter the discussion will be confined to certain key verses of the New Testament which chiefly contain the Bible's teaching on these matters.

CHAPTER IV

THE PURPOSE OF THE
NEW TESTAMENT MIRACLES

Scholarly studies* have been made of the purpose of the miracles. On one point all commentators are agreed. When our Lord saw the crowds, he was emotionally affected, as portrayed in such phrases as Jesus 'when He saw the crowds, he had compassion on them, because they were harassed and helpless, like sheep without a shepherd'.† This was not only because of their sin and unbelief. He was clearly moved by compassion by the evidence of the physical handicaps and the mental suffering of the people whom He saw before Him.

A similar attitude was shown by the Apostles and the evangelists, as described in the Acts. Their later healing miracles appear similarly to have arisen from the motive of compassion. It is worth noting, therefore, that such an attitude towards the sick contrasted sharply with that which was usual amongst the Greeks and the Romans. In classical times the public almost worshipped the streamlined physique of the athlete, and despised, and neglected, the weak or disabled. Compassion early became one of the hall-marks of the Christian faith.

But this motive of compassion is not the only clue in the Gospels to the purpose of the healing miracles. Others which have attracted the notice of scholars will be mentioned (pp. 38-41). There is, however, a central passage which demands more than passing notice.

The Recognition of the Messiah

In Luke 7:18-35 (with the parallel passage in Matthew 11:2-19) there is an account of John the Baptist's sending to Jesus a question about His identity. John himself was at the time in prison and,

---

* *The Miracles of Jesus.* H. Van der Loos, 1905 Leiden: Brill; Morton T. Kelsey: *Healing and Christianity*: In Ancient Thought and Modern Times, 1973 S.C.M.; M. A. H. Melinsky, *Healing Miracles*, 1968, Mowbray.

† Matt. 9:36; 14:14.

perhaps, anticipating the worst. He had been hearing of Jesus' miracles, but because of Christ's delay in claiming the throne of David's kingdom, he had sent two messengers to ask Him if He were really the long-awaited Messiah of Israel of whom he (John) had earlier prophesied. Jesus, instead of simply sending back John's messengers with an affirmative answer, gave them a sign. The account reads: 'At that very time Jesus cured many who had diseases, sicknesses and evil spirits, and gave sight to many who were blind. So he replied to the messengers, "Go back and report to John what you have seen and heard: the blind receive sight, the lame walk, those who have leprosy are cured, the deaf hear, the dead are raised, and the good news is preached to the poor. Blessed is the man who does not fall away on account of Me." ' The point of the actions and the message was that in the Old Testament prophecies of the coming Deliverer, scenes like those taking place were echoing Isaiah's actual words,* which the Lord appears to be quoting.

The natural inference from this context is that a fundamental reason for the association of healing with our Lord's ministry was as an authentication of His being the long expected Messiah. His other miracles, turning water into wine, feeding five thousand people from a few loaves and fish, and calming a storm, demonstrated His control over Nature. But His control over disease brought home the significance of His supernatural powers to the individual and the community.

The Terminology Used in the Greek Text

One series of studies† by a Cambridge New Testament Seminar, led by Professor C. F. D. Moule, has demonstrated convincingly that the main purpose of the miracles in the New Testament was to serve as 'signs'. Throughout the Gospels and the Acts the descriptions of miraculous events are in keeping with the general message and attitude to miracles of the Bible as a whole. The writers chose their words with care‡ and (to describe the miracles)

---

* Isaiah 35: 5-6 and 61:1-3. Compare also, Isaiah 53:4, where it is said that God's servant would take up their infirmities and carry their sorrows.

† *Miracles: Cambridge Studies in their Philosophy and History.* Edited C. F. D. Moule. 1965. London. Mowbray. The most useful sections for our present purpose are Prof. Moule's own Introduction and two Appendices, and Prof. G. W. H. Lampe 'Miracles in the Acts'.

‡ C. F. D. Moule, op. cit.

the choices in the Greek version fell on *dunamis* (a 'power') and *semeion* (a 'sign'), rather than—except for one or two exceptions—on *thauma* (a 'marvel') or *teras* (a 'portent'). The exceptions (where these two last terms are used together) come in contexts which summarise the total situation, such as in the phrase 'signs and *wonders*'. The consistent attitude of the New Testament writers to the miracles—including those of healing—was that these were given as 'signs' of the nature and status of the Person of Christ. The miracles do not stand on their own, they are pointers.

Interest also attaches to the Greek verbs which have been translated into English as 'to heal' or 'to make whole'. These again seem to have been carefully selected by the writers in order to fit the various types of disease and the particular circumstances. * Three verbs are used—*therapeuo*, which emphasises the work of healing; *iaomai*, which places the accent on the powers of the Healer; and *sozo*, which tends to be a much stronger word to convey the concept of a total rescue from peril and, often, of 'salvation'. By far the commonest use of *sozo* is in a spiritual sense applying to man's eternal salvation from sin, but several times it is used of the deliverance of someone who had been seriously ill. There is a practical message for Christians underlying the verb *therapeuo*. For it literally implies 'serving' (as in a household), 'waiting upon', or 'caring'. In two places it describes the activity of domestic servants.† The concept behind the second verb is close to the meaning of *ischuo*, which conveys the thought of 'be strong', 'powerful', or to 'have meaning' or 'validity'. In most of the instances where the Lord appears to be specially asserting His authority as the Messiah, the word *iaomai* has been selected to describe those particular acts of physical healing.

Further, the verb *sozo* is found in most of those incidents where the occurrence of healing is followed by such comments as 'Your faith has saved you; go in peace'. It may, therefore, not be without significance that, in the key New Testament passage of James 5:15, concerning 'the prayer of faith' for a sick person, the word employed is *sozo*. It is possible that the writer's interest

---

* C. G. Scorer—'Another Look at the Healing Miracles', where a number of examples of the use of these terms were given. *In the Service of Medicine* No. 41 (April 1965). E.g. *therapeuo* Matt.4: 23,24; 14:14; *Iaomai*—Luke 5:17; 6:17,19; Acts 10:38; *sozo*—Mark 10:47; Luke 17:12-19; Mark 5:25ff; Luke 8:43ff.

† Luke 12:42 and Matt. 24:45.

here may have been *primarily* in the spiritual welfare of the sick person.*

The Nature of the Cures

The descriptions of most of the healing miracles in the Gospels convey an impression of a finality. As most biblical commentaries point out, one of the chief features of St. Mark's accounts of the healings is his emphasis on the completeness and speed of the result. For him, the only word really strong enough was *euthus*. This can be used as an adjective meaning 'straight' or 'direct', or an adverb 'straightway' or 'immediately'. The other Gospel writers write of the miracles of healing in much the same manner.

It is, however, St. Luke who is more concerned with the medical details of the miracles. This trait in Luke's witness attracted the interest of W. K. Hobart† who analysed the descriptive phrases in the Greek text of the Gospels and the Acts to show that Luke, a physician, was using some of the current medical terminology later popularised by the school of Galen. Whilst more recent scholars regard Hobart as having somewhat overstated his case concerning the extent to which Luke has used technical medical terminology, yet, with reservations his general finding is accepted. A similar study of St. Luke is that by the outstanding American biblical scholar—A. T. Robertson.‡ He impressively demonstrates the historical reliability and care with which St. Luke's Gospel and the Acts have been written. He confirms their value, particularly in reporting the miracles of healing.

Miracles by the Apostles

Hence, in view of St. Luke's accuracy in this respect, we can accept with confidence the descriptions of the miracles found in the Acts of the Apostles. They will be found listed in the Appendix III (p. 97). Some of these obviously compare with those

---

* Readers who wish to follow up these aspects of the Study, should see the articles on these and other related N.T. terms in *The Theological Dictionary of the New Testament.* Ed. Gerhard Kittel. Translated and Edited: Geofrey Bromiley. Eerdmans (1965 and over several dates). The reader should also compare Prof. Tasker's suggestions on this verse, pages 42, 43.

† *The Medical Language of St. Luke.* W. K. Hobart. 1882. London: Longmans.

‡ *Luke the Historian in the Light of Research.* A. T. Robertson. 1920. Edinburgh: T. & T. Clark.

in the Gospels. For example, the healing of the lame man at the
Beautiful Gate of the Temple and the raising of Dorcas. The
further question, therefore, arises concerning the purpose of such
incidents (as recorded in the Acts) in which the Apostles are those
who performed miracles. Why were the Apostles allowed to
demonstrate healing miracles similar to those which were
performed by the Master?

The Gospels provide several clues to the reason for this
extension. When the Apostles were first called into association
with Christ, it is said that He 'gave them power against unclean
spirits, to cast them out, and to heal all manner of sickness and
all manner of disease'.* He then commissioned them to go as
itinerant missionaries with the command to preach in every town
and village that would receive them that 'The kingdom of heaven
is at hand',† whilst He Himself went to certain other cities 'to
teach and preach'.‡ The Apostles' duty at this time was,
therefore, to preach the same message as that of our Lord's—that
the Kingdom of Heaven had now come amongst them, and to call
on Israel to repent, believe and enter the Kingdom. In the
following chapter (of Matthew) it records that 'He began to
upbraid the cities wherein most of His mighty works had been
done',§ because they had not repented and come to Him. One
of the first open invitations of the Gospel, to all mankind, was then
given by Christ—'Come unto Me all ye that labour and are
heavy laden and I will give you rest'.‖ Hence the Twelve were
already being sent as emissaries to convey to a widening public
in the villages His message. There is also a hint of the coming
time when at Pentecost the invitation would be to all the nations.

A little later the influence of these apostolic preachers was
supplemented by the commissioning of a greater number of
itinerant 'missionaries'. 'After this the Lord appointed seventy-
two others and sent them two and two ahead of Him to every
town and place where He was about to go.'$ In other words,
they were to be 'advance parties', (for 'the Harvest truly is great').
It is more important still to note that the *purpose* of the healing
miracles is clearly stated: 'Tell them the kingdom of God is near
you'. At the close of their mission, when on their return they

* Matt. 10:1.   § Matt. 11:20,21.
† Matt. 10:7 and 8.   ‖ Matt. 11:28-30.
‡ Matt. 11:1. $ Luke 10:1.

were congratulating themselves on their results, the Lord's
comment was in the nature of a rebuke: 'Do not rejoice that the
spirits submit to you, but rejoice that your names are written in
heaven'.* Thereby was emphasised that it was not the power
which they were exercising that primarily mattered, or the results
they had achieved, but their own spiritual relationship with their
Master. Then, as if more strongly to emphasise this point, when
the crowds began to assemble in great numbers throughout
Galilee and the disciples reported to Jesus that 'Everyone is
looking for you' (i.e. in order to be healed), He pointedly replies
'Let us go somewhere else—to the nearby villages—so that I can
preach there also. That is why I have come.' In other words,
miracles of healing were continually subordinated to His main
purpose, which was—as King and Saviour—to bring the Gospel
to His people.

How far, it may be asked, did the Apostles in themselves
possess powers of healing? As described in the Gospels, Christ
Himself possessed supernatural therapeutic powers as an integral
part of His presentation of Himself as the Messiah. In the case
of the Apostles and the Seventy, such powers are described as
being *delegated* for the particular preaching tasks assigned to them.
Within the Gospels, at least, we do not read that the disciples
performed miracles apart from such *ad hoc* commissionings.

When we come to the Acts, there are records of several group
healings (see page 19) with a common factor linking them with
those in the Gospels. The Church was in process of being
founded on 'the apostles and prophets, with Christ Jesus Himself
as the chief Corner-stone'.† Peter was destined—at Pentecost—
to be the instrument to open the Kingdom of Heaven to the
Gentiles. The subsequent apostolic preaching missions, including
those of the evangelists Stephen and Philip, were accompanied by
the recognised 'signs' which authenticated their mission. It is to
be noted that the prayer on the lips of the Apostles, when asking
God for a miracle of healing, was 'Stretch out your hand to heal
and perform miraculous signs and wonders through the name of
your holy servant Jesus'.‡ The Jewish observers were looking
'for signs'. Such signs authenticated the apostolic Gospel—just
as there had also been special authentication for the tasks of Elijah

---

* Luke 10:17-20.   ‡ Acts 4:30.
† Ephesians 2:20.

and Elisha at the outset of the age of the prophets. The accounts in the Acts describe the results of the Apostles' preaching and healings as—'Everyone was filled with awe' (2:43) and 'when the crowds heard Philip and saw the miraculous signs which he did, they all payed close attention to what he said' (8:6).

Spiritual Gifts

In the letters of St. Paul there are four lists of 'gifts' possessed by those serving the infant Churches. Two of the lists are in I Corinthians 12:8-10 and 23-30, and the others in Romans and Ephesians respectively.* Some of the series are shared by all four lists, but it is only I Corinthians 12 which mentions healing. Also, this in the Greek text is in the form of a double plural—'gifts of healings'. It is difficult to decide the exact reason for the two plurals, 'gifts of healings'. Attention has been devoted to this phrase in commentaries. One view is that each person possessing such a gift was able to help in the case of a particular disease (or group of diseases), but that he was not necessarily equally effective for all other conditions. In other words, 'each illness requires a special charisma'.† Most of the expositors and Bible translators, however, tend to take the phrase in a general sense, that is, that there were a number of persons who possessed gifts of healing.

If, however, this gift became at all widespread in later apostolic times, as has earlier been commented, it is surprising that (apart from these two general allusions in I Corinthians) there is no further mention of it in the New Testament! It is even a greater matter for surprise that St. Paul should suggest 'a little wine' for Timothy's gastritis,‡ that he should leave Trophimus unwell at Miletus,§ and that he reports that Epaphroditus had been critically ill before being sent back to the Philippians.‖ Paul himself also writes that he has had permanently to reconcile himself to his 'thorn in the flesh', whatever this may have been.$ In summary, the economy of detail in references to this matter in the New Testament, and the contexts in which they occur, suggest that the healing gifts were primarily associated with the

---

* See pages 19 and 97.
† I Corinthians: Robertson & Plummer (I.C.C.) and F. W. Grosheede (N.I.C. of the N.T.).
‡ I Tim. 5:23.   ‖ Phil. 2:30.
§ II Tim. 4:20. $ II Cor. 12:7.

Messiah's own *preaching* tours, and subsequently also of those of the apostolic missionaries.

The Chief New Testament Passage

The central reference in Scripture to faith healing is in the Epistle of James 5:13-20. The New International Version translates: 'Is any one of you sick? He should call the elders of the church to pray over him and anoint him with oil in the name of the Lord. And the prayer offered in faith will make the sick person well; the Lord will raise him up. If he has sinned, he will be forgiven. Therefore confess your sins to each other, and pray for each other, so that you may be healed. The prayer of a righteous man is powerful and effective.' The context of this statement—with its explanatory comment before and after—is that of intercessory prayer. It is a special prayer meeting. Associated with the situation in this passage is also the confession of 'sins'.

J. W. R. Stott has suggested one practical explanation for this recommendation to call the elders. A very ill patient may find it (indeed, many when gravely ill in hospital, or at home do find it) difficult to pray. A seriously ill or comatose patient, of course, cannot pray for himself. So whether called by the sufferer or his relatives, the representatives of the Christian congregation may be called in for the purpose of intercession on his behalf. It is something which the Church does corporately for the sick in time of need. If he has particular 'sins' on his conscience, the sick person is encouraged to unburden himself to the elders. The context does not suggest that the latter in themselves have any special powers. It is the Lord Who 'will raise him up'.

Professor R. V. G. Tasker* in his commentary on the Epistle has several relevant comments—'The description of the elders' prayer as "*the prayer of faith*" does not differentiate it from other kinds of prayer, for there can be no Christian prayer at all without faith. Much current teaching in the contemporary Church on the subject of "spiritual healing" rests on the false assumption that it is God's will that everybody should enjoy at all times perfect physical health. There is nothing in the New Testament to justify the assumption, and some evidence points in the opposite direction.'

* *James*: R. V. G. Tasker 1956.   Tyndale Commentaries.

He continues 'The expression *shall save*, in the context, must mean "shall restore to physical health"; for the New Testament nowhere asserts that men are saved, in a spiritual sense, by prayer.' Also, Professor Tasker goes on to point out that the Greek word used for the sick person, *ton kamnonta*, is the present participle of a verb whose primary meaning is 'to grow weary', having a secondary sense of growing weary by reason of sickness. It is improbable that it is intended to suggest that the sufferer is dying. Similarly, the use of *egerei* in the expression 'shall raise him up', suggests that it is not a spiritual resurrection, but getting up from his bed.

Anointing with Oil

Concerning the suggested use of oil, the late Professor Rendle Short* comments that whether it was a 'ritual' or 'remedial' anointing cannot be determined from the text. He comments: 'Two Greek words are translated "anoint", *aleipho* and *chrio*. In James the word is *aleipho*. When a symbolical or ceremonial anointing is meant, *chrio* is normally used . . . but when the woman anointed our Lord's feet with ointment, *aleipho* is used. In classical Greek the rubbing of an athlete's limbs with oil was similarly described. In the Greek version of the Old Testament, *aleipho* occurs seventeen times but is used in a ceremonial sense in only two of these. It may, therefore, well be that the anointing with oil in James, and Mark†, was remedial rather than ceremonial. . . . The ancients used external medicaments freely. However, there is room for difference of opinion.'

Some writers, notably H. W. Frost,‡ argue that because the rest of the Apostles are silent on the subject, the use of oil would appear to be 'permissive, but not mandatory'. There are only two other references in the New Testament to the use of oil, first by the Good Samaritan where plainly it is intended to be medicinal and, then, in Mark 6:13, where during the special mission of the Apostles 'They drove out many devils, and many sick people they anointed with oil and cured'. The evidence suggests that the Epistle of James is one of the earliest New Testament books. It would seem that in the time of the Gospels and the early days of

* *The Bible and Modern Medicine.* A. Rendle Short. 1953. Paternoster Press.
† Mark 6:13.
‡ *Miraculous Healing.* H. W. Frost. 1951. Marshall, Morgan and Scott.

the Church, when James was writing, the use of oil (which is more
in keeping with the Old Testament outlook) was still being
practised. Since there is no additional reference to the practice
in the New Testament it may have fallen into disuse.

The chief inference, therefore, from the New Testament's
teaching on healing would seem to be that—in keeping with the
exhortation 'in *everything* by prayer and petition, with thanksgiving,
present your requests to God'*—the Christian should bring
matters of health and sickness to God in prayer. When he is
seriously ill—and, so finds it difficult to pray for himself—he is
advised to call for the representatives of the Church to come to
pray with him and on his behalf. If his conscience is troubled
because of sins (the Greek word is plural) he is encouraged to
unburden himself to these Elders. But 'all power' or 'authority'
remains in the hands of the Lord of the Church. It is the Lord
who 'will raise him up'. The central lesson is the duty of the
members of the Church to pray for one another and, in the
context of this passage in James, we are taught the importance
and effectiveness of such corporate intercession.

* Philippians 4:6.

Chapter V

FAITH HEALING IN HISTORY

A full review of the historical evidence for, or against, the continuance of miraculous healing in the Church would require much space. Attention would also need to be given to the precise relevance of such material as is available in the writings of the early Fathers. A good deal of misunderstanding, and probably error, has arisen from the different ways in which various writers have selected from the documents and evaluated them. All that can be attempted here is to refer to several crucial points. Throughout the history of the non-Christian religions, modern cults and even some secular organizations there have been claims to various forms of 'spiritual' or 'mind' healing. The results have usually been interpreted by the disciples of the respective religion, or movement, as authenticating its distinctive outlook.

In Greek and Secular History

In early Greece two traditions can be traced which have parallels in other regions of the Near East. The Ebers Papyrus—a very early medical document from Egypt (1550 B.C.)—makes clear that, in addition to the temples where various religious rituals were carried out in the treatment of disease, there were proto-types of the later schools of medical thought and training. In most parts of the Eastern Mediterranean this dual process is in evidence—there is scientific rationalising of the art of healing, whilst at the same time claiming some of the gods as patrons of the healing processes. Of the latter Aesculapius—a son of Zeus—became the best known. The gods of healing were thought of as mediators between Zeus and mankind in matters of health. In popularity as a place of pilgrimage Epidauros would seem to have been an ancient forerunner of Lourdes. In later times some of the Roman Emperors were credited with 'divine' healing powers. Vespasian and Hadrian were reputed to have cured the lame and the blind. Adherence to religious forms of cures for disease continued into later centuries alongside the more professional applications of the collection of Hippocratic (and, later, of Galenic) medical knowledge. A complete account would need to trace the influence of these early non-Christian healing centres in the Grecco-Roman world* and to follow the growth of various magico-religious cults down through the Dark Ages and into mediaeval times.

The story would also need to include a number of individual 'natural' healers at later periods, for example, Valentine Great-rakes, known as the 'Stroker'—because of his method of laying hands on his 'patients' in the Seventeenth Century. There was also the process of 'touching for the King's Evil', a practice carried out by the Tudor and Caroline monarchs in which they 'touched' large numbers of people suffering from scrofula and gave them a gold coin. In 1684 a Surgeon, John Brown, reported that some 90,000 persons had been 'touched' between 1660 and 1682. He had carefully examined 50 of these, and sifted the evidence, and he accepted that some of these persons appeared definitely to have been healed.†

Further, a complete survey would add a considerable number of individual healers, cults and movements which in recent times have made their contribution to what has become known as 'Fringe Medicine'. These include Christian Science practitioners, together with other types of 'mind cure', the mediums of Spiritualist healers,‡ and the application of sophisticated physical 'forces', such as that known as radiaesthesia. The aim in this chapter, however, is to consider such Christian claims as have been made during Church History.

The Early Church Fathers

The chief barriers to an exhaustive examination of the writings of the early Fathers is their great volume § and, second, ideally the need to examine them in their original Greek and Latin. How far those who have produced theses, books and articles on this

---

* See the histories of Medicine; for example: F. H. Garrison (1929); H. Sigerist (1961); A. H. Underwood and C. Singer (1962). Also the *Medical Background of Anglo-Saxon England*: W. Bonsor; *The Mediaeval Hospitals of England*: R. Clay (1928), and *Mediaeval and Renaissance Medicine*: B. L. Gordon (1959).

† *The Book of Miracles*: George Fox, 1928.   ‡ See page 11.

§ The editions of Jacques Paul Migre's *Patrologiae Cursus Completus* run to a series of large volumes of which there are 221 in the Latin series and 161 in the Greek series.

subject have been able to examine this vast corpus of literature at first-hand is not clear. In 1940 Dr. Evelyn Frost included in her London University thesis translated extracts from the Ante-Nicene Fathers.* Amongst the references provided there, the most relevant to our present purpose would seem to be those from Irenaeus in his *Against Heresies* (about A.D. 185), Tertuliian in *On the Soul* (about 210) and Origen in *Against Celsus* (about 247). It seems a fair comment that the total result of the searches for reports of healing in patristic literature is not nearly as impressive as one might have anticipated. Few of the extracts seem to indicate that the writers were themselves personally acquainted with any of the somewhat vaguely reported healing events. They had '*heard*' of them.†

It also seems significant that an extract quoted by Eusebius from the Apology of Quadratus, written about A.D. 124 and which is regarded as the earliest known book of Christian Apologetics, does not refer to any *contemporary* healings. The writer refers back to Christ's miracles as one line in the evidence for the truth of the Christian Faith. He writes 'Our Saviour's works . . . were always present: for they were real, those who had been healed of their diseases, those who had been raised from the dead; who were not only seen whilst they were being healed and raised up, but were constantly present. Nor did they remain only during the sojourn of our Saviour (on earth), but also a considerable time after His departure; and, indeed, some of them have survived even down to our own times.' The impression on the reader is that Quadratus was looking back to what was distinctive of the Apostolic age, and indicating that only a few of the witnesses from apostolic times were still alive.

It is often not easy to be sure whether the various Fathers are, like Quadratus, referring to the past era of the Gospels (much as Hebrews Chapter XI recounts the deeds of the Old Testament heroes of the Faith) or to miracles reported as having been witnessed by their immediate predecessors or their contemporaries. But Irenaeus, when castigating the heretics against whom he is writing, asserts the fact that they cannot 'confer sight on the blind, hearing on the deaf, nor chase away all sorts of demons. . . . And

---

* On pages 64-110 and the Appendix, pages 249-267 of *Christian Healing*, Evelyn Frost.

† Page 24.

so far are they from being able to raise the dead, as the Lord raised
them, and the Apostles by means of prayer, and as has been done
frequently in the brotherhood on account of some necessity . . . that
they do not even believe that it can possibly be done.' The
reference to 'the brotherhood' seems to make the claim that there
had been such events in the Church since the time of the Apostles.

In a similar manner, Origen writes in the Third Century that
'There are still preserved among the Christians traces of that Holy
Spirit which appeared in the form of a dove. They expel evil
spirits and perform many cures, and foresee certain events,
according to the will of the Logos.' He also writes that the Jews
'have no longer prophets nor miracles, traces of which to a
considerable extent are still found amongst Christians, and some
of them are more remarkable than any that existed among the
Jews; and these we ourselves have witnessed.' The word *'traces'*
does not argue a very widespread occurrence of the happenings
which are mentioned. In another place he speaks of a 'growing
scarcity of miracles' and 'There were signs from the Holy Spirit
at the beginning of Christ's teaching, and after His ascension He
exhibited more, but subsequently fewer. Nevertheless, even now
still there are traces of them with a few who have had their souls
purified by the Gospel.' The total number of such references so
far found in the writings of the Fathers are fewer and less convinc-
ing than are needed to enable the reader to be sure that the
Apostolic and Ante-Nicene Fathers were familiar with numerous
contemporary cases of healing.

An Unanswered Critique

In his study of the problem mentioned on page 24, the late Professor B. B. Warfield has called attention to an Eighteenth Century
polemic written by a somewhat sceptical—Gibbons type of—
writer Conyers Middleton.* His book bore the extensive title
'*A Free Enquiry into the Miraculous Powers*, which are supposed to
have subsisted in the Christian Church from the earliest ages
through several successive centuries; tending to show that we have
no sufficient reason to believe on the authority of the primitive
fathers, that any such powers were continued to the Church after
the days of the Apostles' (London 1747). Its thesis is that the
writings of the Fathers do not bear out the historical claim that

* *Miracles: Yesterday and To-day.* B. B. Warfield 1918 (reprinted 1965).

healing miracles, such as recorded in the New Testament, continued in a similar manner after the death of the last Apostle. This contribution is written in trenchant Eighteenth Century prose and is an able piece of work which cannot be ignored. Up until the year 1918 when he was writing, Warfield states that, though there had since been a number of careful searches into the Patristic literature and efforts to vindicate the opposing view (that is, that the apostolic type of miracle had continued into later Church History), yet, 'after a century and a half the book remains unrefuted, and, indeed, despite the faults arising from the writer's spirit, and the limitations inseparable from the state of scholarship in his day, its main contention seems to be put beyond dispute'.

In a similar manner, J. S. McEwen* writes 'The question is one of historic fact. If the Early Church possessed a great ministry of healing and lost it through unbelief, there is no obvious reason why that ministry should not be restored in full measure to men of faith today; indeed there can be no excuse for failure to revive the lost ministry. If, however, it cannot be shown that the Early Church once possessed and gradually forfeited this ministry, then the modern Church must view with considerable caution and reserve the efforts of those who are seeking to give it a leading place in the Church today.' He proceeds to examine the statements of Justin Martyr, Tertullian, Irenaeus and Origen. He found that by far the greater number of references to such things in the Second and Third Centuries seem not to be about physical healing at all, but refer to means of counteracting the forces of evil, and the exorcism of evil spirits. McEwen concludes: 'What the Early Church chiefly lamented was the decline of its spectacular success in exorcisms'.

The Dark Ages and the Mediaeval Church

The records make clear, however, that from the Fourth Century right on until the time of the Reformation, an immense literature of hagiography developed and there were many accounts of spectacular 'miracles'. Marvels were reported associated with the lives of saints, their relics and particular holy places. The majority of the leading theologians, preachers and ecclesiastics of the period accepted readily the accounts of such marvels and

* The Ministry of Healing. J. S. McEwen. *Scottish Journal of Theology*, Vol. 7, No. 2. 1954.

'miracles' of these times. Of Bernard of Clairvaux, Gibbon wrote:
'It may seem remarkable that Bernard who records so many
miracles of his friend, St. Malachi, never takes any notice of his
own, which in their turn, however, are carefully related by his
companions and disciples. In the long series of reports of
miraculous happenings in ecclesiastical history, does there exist
a single instance of a saint asserting that he himself possessed the
gift of performing miracles?' Its absence might, of course, be
due to the saintly practice of a due modesty. It might, however,
be due to the fact that the writers themselves had little *personal* experience of these things and were reporting the experience of others.

Warfield has also drawn attention to the differing attitudes
amongst 19th Century Christian leaders to the question of the
Mediaeval 'miracles'. He, especially discusses a significant
change in the views of Henry Newman in the latter part of his life.
As a post-graduate student in Oxford Newman had in 1825-6
written a paper, when he was a Protestant, entitled *The Miracles
of Scripture*, 'as compared with those elsewhere, as regards their
nature, credibility and evidence'. This was strongly critical of
ecclesiastical miracles. In 1842-3, however, a second essay was
written, after he had become a Roman Catholic. This has the
altered title of *The Miracles of Ecclesiastical History* ('compared with
those of Scripture, as regards their nature, credibility and
evidence'). This second essay is a plea for the reality of the whole
accumulation of reported ecclesiastical miracles in the Middle
Ages! The result must be regarded as a masterpiece of special
pleading based on a subtle alteration in the emphasis. As
Warfield says: 'After he has, under the cover of candour, concentrated attention upon what seem to him the particular miracles
most deserving to be true, and supported by the most direct and
weighty evidence, he subtly suggests that, on their basis, many
more (in themselves) doubtful or distasteful may be allowed, that
insufficiency of proof is not the same as disproof, and that very
many things must be admitted by us to be very likely true, for the
truth of which we have no evidence at all—inasmuch as we must
distinguish sharply between the fact and the proof of the fact, and
must be prepared to admit that failure of the latter does not carry
with it the rejection of the former!'

There is a good deal of somewhat similar reasoning today, and
it tends to proceed along similar lines. But, we must ask, does

such an attitude do God a service—if, in fact, the reality of the phenomena claimed is not supported by reliable evidence and credible witnesses?

The Era of the Reformation and the Eighteenth Century

It is unfortunately true that in several ways the radical changes which came about during the Renaissance and Reformation tended for a time to make things worse for the infirm and seriously ill. The dissolution of the monasteries and nunneries greatly reduced the number of hospices to which in some localities had been attached what were, in effect, our earliest and rudimentary hospitals. In some communities, however, the civic corporations —as in the case of the City of London, which was persuaded to adopt St. Bartholomew's—undertook responsibility for maintaining some of the hospices on a somewhat secularised basis. In places where the Church had retained a strong link with a hospice there are, here and there, embedded in the records a few reports of what may have been cases of faith healing.

In Reformation times one dramatic account came from the Continent, where James Welch—John Knox's son-in-law—was in exile. He had been compelled to flee to France after attending an unlawful assembly which had been suppressed by the authorities in Aberdeen. The papers of the Woodrow Society include a letter in which Welch writes from St. Jean d'Angely as if he had been the means of the resurrection from the dead of a young fellow-countryman. Subsequently in Scotland there was a widespread tradition to this effect. But Young's *Life of John Welch* reports the incident as follows: 'Two young gentlemen from Scotland were boarded with him for their education. One of them was the Master of Ochiltree. To him Welch refers in the postscript of a letter to Boyd of Trochrig. "The young man, our cousin, is here, of whom I shall have a singular care, if it please the Lord." Concerning this youth, a tradition was handed down to the effect that, falling sick of a lingering and grievous distemper, he died, but was miraculously brought again to life by the effectual fervent prayer of his affectionate host. The episode, as recorded by Kirkston, is long and minute, but not very edifying. By certain parties it has been made a handle of for casting reproach on the memory of Welch, on serious religion, and on the cause of Presbytery.'

'But, let it be observed in the first place that Welch never pretended to be endowed with the power of working miracles, or of raising the dead to life.   Secondly, the marvellous narrative rests upon no more solid foundation than a popular tradition, which in the course of transmission has evidently received numerous and incredible additions.   The amount of the whole, we believe, is simply this—that having "a singular care" of his young and noble relative, Welch earnestly prayed for his recovery, and it pleased the Sovereign Arbiter of life and death to listen to his supplications for the recovery of the youth when at the point of death.   And who but an infidel will deny that the "effectual, fervent prayer of a righteous man availeth much", in modern as well as in ancient times?'

During the Covenanting period in Scotland there were also several reports of the unexpected recovery from critical illness and physical injury amongst the itinerant ministers who were being sought by the Government troops.   Similarly, during times of the spiritual revivals—especially those of the Eighteenth Century— there were a few similar reports.   In the outlook of the outstanding Evangelical leader of the Eighteenth Century, John Wesley, there are two elements.   He shows in all circumstances his customary unbounded faith in God.   He clearly believed in, and practised, the most earnest intercession for those Christians who were ill— though, so far as is known, he did not make a doctrine of 'faith healing' or make any healing claims.   At the same time, he applied his robust common sense to medical treatment and compiled for his circuit-ministers and lay preachers, what (for that age) was one of the most practical handbooks of medical treatment available.   Whilst it included some of the dubious polypharmacy and nostrums of the day, Wesley's *Primitive Physick* contains much good counsel.   It could be regarded as the proto-type of the family Medical Encyclopaedias of more recent times.   Indeed, Wesley has good claim to be regarded as one of the earliest advocates of hygiene and public health in this country.

The Nineteenth Century

Perhaps the earliest ad hoc investigation in Britain into the question of the Charismatic gifts—particularly of healing and 'speaking in languages'—was undertaken about the year 1830 by Edward Irving, whose associates later founded the Catholic Apostolic

Church. Irving himself made several journeys from London to Scotland to investigate reports concerning the experiences of a gifted young woman, Mary Campbell, living on a farm near Garelochhead, and also of James Macdonald in Port Glasgow. During a local religious revival, Mary Campbell, who was expected soon to die from advanced tuberculosis, was engaged in prayer with some friends one Sunday evening in March 1830, when she began to speak in an unknown language, and was believed to have received the 'gift of tongues'. Shortly after she rose from her bed, married and lived a fairly normal life until her death in 1840. Round about the same date at Port Glasgow, James MacDonald one lunch-time returned to his home to find that the rest of the family was gathered around his 'invalid' sister, who was in a state of spiritual turmoil and whom they believed to be dying. But she revived and welcomed him, praying that he would receive the gift of the Holy Spirit. Immediately he exclaimed 'I have got it' and his first act was to take her by the hand and to call on her in the words of Psalm 20 to 'arise and stand upright'. She at once did this and threw off the restraints of her illness.* These cases—with several others, together with the experience of some of their own members in London—formed the immediate basis of the claim amongst Irving's congregation in the Regent's Square Church that there had been a restoration to the Church of what were believed to be the apostolic 'charismatic gifts'. The subsequent history of this movement, however, was not at all plain sailing. These sincere Christian seekers were destined to meet with many problems and disappointments, including (soon after his expulsion from the Presbyterian ministry) the marked decline in the formerly brilliant Edward Irving's preaching powers and his early death.

Throughout the rest of the Nineteenth Century there remained a few small groups and isolated individuals who, from time to time, advocated 'faith healing' and reported individual cases. It was not, however, until after the beginning of the present Century that there began an extensive new interest. This came with the arrival of the first Pentecostal missionaries from North America in 1906 and 1907. This original Pentecostal mission has in recent years been supplemented—and in some areas replaced—by later new initiatives associated with successful evangelists and

* No precise medical diagnosis at the time was given and hysteria is not excluded.

the 'Charismatic Movement' within some of the main denomina-
tions.

Lourdes

Officially the Roman Catholic Church has always taken the view
that ecclesiastically, as in all other respects, the authority and
special powers of the Apostles were in fact passed down in history
to the contemporary Pope, who claims to be the successor of St.
Peter.   It is, therefore, no accident that in the areas where the
Roman Catholic Church has predominated, there have for
centuries been shrines, relics of the saints and wells which are said
to have inherited and preserved healing powers of the apostolic
kind.   The most popular of these in modern times has been the
Grotto at Lourdes, which is still visited annually by thousands of
pilgrims.   It began as a place of healing from the time in 1858
when a country girl of 14 years of age reported the appearance to
her of the Virgin Mary as 'a girl in white, no bigger than me'.
From that time the list of favours granted to those visiting the
grotto and accounts of supernatural happenings, bringing healing
to those in physical need, have grown to large numbers.   It is
said that by 1908 (the 50th anniversary of its becoming a place of
pilgrimage) over 10,000,000 persons had visited Lourdes.   In
modern times, with the greater ease of modern transport, the total
numbers must by now have exceeded accurate computation.
Many claims have been made to healing and the crutches of those
no longer lame have been left at the grotto.   It is difficult for
uncommitted observers to be certain what the total results have
really been.   There are, however, official reports issued by the
Canonical Commission, and individual claims to healing are also
monitored by a special Medical Bureau in Paris.   Their views will
be considered in Chapters VI and VII amongst the medical
evidence.

The Twentieth Century

In Britain comprehensive studies of this whole matter awaited
the aftermath of the First World War.   Just before it Percy
Dearmer in 1909 had led the way by publishing what was the
first of a number of individual surveys of the subject.*   At the
close of the War, when various forms of reconstruction were being

* *Body and Soul.*   Percy Dearmer, 1909.

pressed forward, the question of the place of the Christian faith in confronting suffering and disease came to the fore. Several individuals and groups founded organizations and hospices to serve as centres of 'spiritual' healing. These pioneer initiatives rapidly grew in number and size. There are today many such guilds and societies, with well over a hundred hospices and special healing centres. In 1967 the Churches Council of Healing made a survey of these centres and published an outline of the position at that date.*

In all such Christian organizations the basic concept is that the churches must be more fully involved in intercession for the seriously ill. Some go further than others in their use for these purposes of the sacrament of Holy Communion, with the 'Prayer for the Sick' (including anointing with oil). Fundamentally, however, the uniting concept is that of *intercession*. Perhaps this has been seen at its best in the Divine Healing Mission. Begun as a circle for united prayer and intercession, this movement eventually crystallised its activity in a healing centre at Crowhurst, Sussex.†

An examination of the history of the healing movements in the various Churches underlines the place and importance of prayer in the presence of suffering. The Bible itself has encouraged us 'in everything by prayer and petition with thanksgiving to present our requests to God'.‡ Amongst the common needs are matters of health. But experience suggests caution. The outcome depends upon God. We can never dictate to Him, or presume upon His healing powers. Christian humility and common prudence would suggest that any statements concerning the mystery of physical healing must be restrained. It is part of the discipline of God's children that they should have to live from day to day totally dependent on Him. In response to their prayers and intercessions *He heals when, and as, He pleases.*

* *Guilds and Fellowships of Healing.* The Churches Council of Healing. 1967.
† *Christ Healing.* E. Howard Cobb. 1935. Lakeland. (See also page 77.)
‡ Phil. 4:6.

CHAPTER VI

MEDICAL EVIDENCE FOR
FAITH HEALING

If the total number of claims made by all the centres of 'faith' or 'spiritual' healing could be accepted as they stand, the result would be very impressive. Further discussion would be unnecessary. The fact, however, remains that whenever a medical investigator, or group of medically trained persons, have made a careful and sympathetic search into the reported 'cures', they have had to become increasingly cautious in their assessments.

There are some obvious steps in any controlled professional approach to the various contemporary claims which will suggest themselves to a medical reader. If a well-trained doctor is to be intellectually convinced beyond doubt that a claimed recovery is a true miracle of 'faith healing', he will need data of the kind to which he is used in his daily work. First, he will need to have a reasonably complete *medical* documentation of the case and its diagnosis before the reported visit to the source of healing. An ideal situation would be where a serious disease (or longstanding disability affecting one or more physical structures of the body) was undoubtedly present. Preferably the diagnosis and stage of progress of the disease would have been agreed (before the healing event) by more than one consultant, each of whom was a specialist in that respective group of diseases, and who had been able to confirm the diagnosis by the usual clinical tests. Preferably, also, there would have been no *ad hoc* medical treatment for the condition (or it had been discontinued) for some months before the visit to the 'healer' or healing community.

A further ideal situation would be where the *same* specialists could re-examine the case and repeat the clinical tests after the healing. It would also be ideal that, if possible, the *same* specialists could again see the patient after a sufficiently long interval. This, or something as nearly as possible like it, would be the optimum confirmatory procedure from a medical point of view.

In practice, however, it will seldom prove easy to approach such an ideal. Seriously ill persons about to seek the aid of a 'healer' or 'healing mission' are understandably, and for a variety of reasons, not specially anxious to co-operate in such a procedure. Individual healers and 'healing centres' are also naturally reluctant to be subjected to (what they feel are) 'trials' or 'experiments' by critics, whom they regard as basically unsympathetic. Also the patients' own practitioners, and the hospitals concerned, may not be interested (or for professional reasons willing) to assist. A patient's case notes are strictly speaking the confidential property of the National Health Service or of the respective private practitioners. Other factors increase any observer's difficulty in being able to put together 'a *series*' of cases relevant to such an enquiry.

It is important also to recognise that the leaders of Christian 'healing centres' feel quite sincerely that there is an implied affront to the Divine Healer in any such 'investigation'. They deprecate what they anticipate will be irreverence, pharisaism, or even cynicism on the part of 'incredulous' medically trained workers. These appear to them to wish to call in question the nature, reality or completeness of 'divine miracles'.

Earlier Enquiries in Medical Circles

Evidence of a special interest amongst British doctors began in 1910, when *the British Medical Journal* (June 18) published a series of papers discussing the question of faith healing in relation to the diseases which were resistant to the Medicine of the day. A leading article suggested that there was evidence for believing that cures 'which, in a former day, would have been denied by unbelievers and accepted as miracles by the faithful, really happen, and that they can be explained without invoking supernatural intervention'. Some of the discussion somewhat vaguely anticipates various aspects of subsequent progress in psychiatry. There is evidence also of interest in 'spiritual healing'. In the same year a book was published entitled *Medicine and the Church,** to which several prominent medical men, including Sir Clifford Allbut, at the time the Regius Professor of Physics at Cambridge, Stephen Paget, F.R.C.S. and Charles Butler (a former President of the Harveian Society) contributed. The papers in this symposium refer to the wide-

* *Medicine and the Church.* Edited Geoffrey Rhodes. 1910. Kegan Paul.

spread interest which has been taken of late in what is called 'Spiritual Healing', or 'Healing by Spiritual means'. The primary aim of most of the contributors was to increase co-operation between the Church and Medicine.

Dr. Hugh Trowell* has called attention to a study made in 1914 by Anglican clergy, assisted by doctors, which (due to the First World War 1914-1918) did not at the time receive the attention it deserved.† 'Nine eminent Anglican clerics (a bishop, 3 deans and 5 priests) and 11 eminent doctors' published their findings. The members of this Commission state that they 'are aware that no sharply defined fundamental distinction can be drawn between "organic" (structural changes in organs) and "functional" (that is, no change in structure; but having a psychological cause) ailments. They are forced, however, to the conclusion after the most careful enquiry, that "faith" and "spiritual" healing, like all treatment by suggestion, can be permanently effective only in cases of what are generally termed "functional disorders". The alleged exceptions are so disputable that they cannot be taken into account. . . . They thankfully recognise that persons suffering from organic disease are greatly comforted, and even physically benefited by spiritual ministrations.' Dr. Trowell has also drawn attention to an enquiry in 1920 by Canon Grensted (Oxford) into the results of two 'healing missions' conducted by Anglican clergy. 'Letters sent to every doctor and clergyman in the districts concerned failed to produce any information concerning the real nature of definitely organic cases, though there is plenty of evidence of the cure of functional disorders.'

The British Medical Association's Enquiry

It was not until 1956 that the British Medical Association returned to a more definitely official interest in the subject.‡ It replied in that year to a series of questions put to it by the Archbishop of Canterbury's 'Commission on Divine Healing'. This Commission, containing twelve doctors and nurses, reported later in

* *Study Notes on Faith Healing.* H. Trowell. 1969. Institute of Religion and Medicine.

† *Spiritual Healing.* (Report of Special Committee of Clergy and Doctors.) 1914.

‡ *Divine Healing and Co-operation between Doctors and Clergy.* 1956. B.M.A. Publications.

1958.* The B.M.A's findings were based upon the replies to a well-advertised questionnaire sent to large numbers of doctors and organizations devoted to the task of 'faith' or 'spiritual' healing from a number of different viewpoints. An interviewing committee, chaired by a much respected and fair-minded consultant, met the representatives of a number of these organizations and discussed their submissions. Every effort was made to sift accurately all evidence which contributed to an understanding of the cases.

The B.M.A's Report concluded: 'We find that, whilst patients suffering from psychogenic disorders may be "cured" by various methods of spiritual healing, just as they are by methods of suggestion and other forms of psychological treatment employed by doctors, we can find no evidence that organic diseases are cured solely by such means. The evidence suggests that many such cases claimed to be cured are likely to be either instances of wrong diagnosis, wrong prognosis, remission or possibly of spontaneous cure.† On the other hand, as there are multiple factors—whether of body or mind—which may contribute to the precipitation of an illness, so there are multiple factors which conduce to the restoration of health. . . . Religious ministration, on whatever basis it rests, may have an important bearing upon the emotional and spiritual life of the patient and so contribute to recovery.'

Lourdes

A 'standing committee' of doctors (the Bureau de Constations) has officially been organised for investigating the results of the pilgrimages to Lourdes. The Roman Catholic Church early in their history appointed a Canonical Commission to assess each year's result and to put forward to a committee of doctors (the Bureau) those cases which they considered had qualified to be accepted as true miracles. The Medical Bureau is very strict in the criteria applied to any case which it is prepared to accept. At the outset the Canonical Commission itself requires '1. that the malady should be grave and not improving under medical treatment; 2. that the claimed cure was instantaneous, with no

---

* *The Church's Ministry of Healing.* 1958. Church Information Office.

† For example, almost all types of malignant growth have—though very rarely—been known spontaneously to regress.

period of convalescence; 3. that the cure was perfect and that there was no relapse.' In the first hundred years of the grotto's being a place of pilgrimage the number of such cases put forward by the Commission, and which were accepted by the Medical Bureau de Constations, was fifty-one.

Perhaps the medical requirements are too exacting? The Canonical Commission, judging by the larger numbers which it submits, would appear to be disposed to accept a good many more cases than the Bureau. Even so—if we take the higher figures of the Commission than those accepted by the Bureau— the number of those claimed to have been miraculously cured (in view of the tens of thousands who visit the Grotto) would seem to be very small in proportion. A Methodist minister, the late Dr. Leslie Weatherhead, has described a visit which he made to Lourdes. The effect on him was that he estimated that 98% of the pilgrims annually return to their homes without physical improvement.

The difficulties of arriving at a true assessment of the situation has been illustrated by the description of a case at Lourdes given by Dr. Alexis Carrel.* He saw an 'abdominal tumour' subside as he closely watched the patient. But a similar example used to be mentioned to his students by the late Norman Lake, when he was senior surgeon at Charing Cross Hospital. He would recount how in this case an abdominal mass would appear inter- mittently accompanied by painful episodes. The mass, however, subsided on each occasion during the induction of the anaesthetic in preparation for operation. On the fourth occasion, since the mass had only partially diminished in size, Lake decided to go ahead with laparotomy. He was just in time to see a complete volvulus of the sigmoid colon in process of becoming untwisted. There are a number of such occasions when it is difficult to be quite certain of a diagnosis. Popular descriptions of medical conditions are often, quite unintentionally, very misleading.

Search by Individual Investigators

The late Professor Rendle Short of Bristol several times stated in meetings of medical students that he had searched for years for clear cases of organic disease which had been undoubtedly healed through faith, apart from known medical treatment. His list

* *Journey to Lourdes*. A. Carrel. 1949. Hamish Hamilton.

of possible cases was very small. He would often describe* one case, which had challenged his interest. A life-long sufferer from asthma, at the age of 75 years had gone, after a sleepless night, looking like a dying man to the prayer meeting of his church. The sufferer subsequently described how, on this occasion, soon after the commencement of the prayers, he distinctly heard a voice behind him saying 'I will heal you to-day'. He had immediately jumped to his feet to thank God and the others present joined him in the thanksgiving. When Professor Rendle Short heard from the 'patient' three years later the latter reported that since that meeting there had been no more symptoms or attacks of his asthma.

Another observer, Dr. Louis Rose (a psychiatrist at St. Bartholomew's Hospital, London), over the course of some 15 to 20 years up to 1968, went to considerable lengths in an effort to investigate by means of personal interviews and questionnaires all types of claim to miraculous healing. For example, he had protracted interchanges and interviews with Harry Edwards, the spiritualist healer. He also corresponded with and sought to interview the leaders of various Christian centres and organizations. He resolutely sought to follow up all possible leads, and to keep an open mind. He found—just as others also have found—that by far the majority of the healing centres were unwilling to co-operate in such an enquiry, and that it was with the utmost difficulty that replies could be extracted and sufficient documentation obtained concerning any of the cases. In his book, *Faith Healing*† he states—'I have analyzed 96 instances of purported faith cures and found that—

(i) in 58 cases it was not possible to obtain medical or other records, so that the claims remain unconfirmed.

(ii) In 22 cases, records were so much at variance with the claims that it was considered useless to continue investigating.

(iii) In 2 cases the evidence in the medical records suggested that the healer may have contributed to amelioration of an organic condition.

* *The Bible and Modern Medicine.* A. Rendle Short. 1953. p. 133. Paternoster Press.

† *Faith Healing.* L. Rose. 1968. Victor Gollancz. Quotation is by permission of the publishers, Victor Gollancz Ltd.

(iv) In one case demonstrable organic disability was relieved or cured after intervention by the healer.

(v) 3 cases improved, but relapsed.

(vi) 4 cases showed a satisfactory degree of improvement in function, although re-examination and comparison with medical records revealed no change in the organic state.

(vii) In 5 cases there was improvement when healing was received concurrently with orthodox medical treatment.

(viii) One case, examined by the author himself, before and after treatment by a healer, had received no benefit and continued to deteriorate.'

Dr. Rose concludes 'Broadly, it is possible to take five attitudes towards purported faith cures. One can ignore the entire subject, a course which would seem inadvisable for mankind, as a whole and one which physicians in particular would find hard to justify. One can deny that there are any phenomena worthy of critical attention, a view which would perhaps be reasonable were faith cures as rare as successful alchemists. One can uncritically accept that paranormal forces intervene in affairs of human health, or one can equally uncritically assume that any and every example of the healer's art will be found explicable through considerations of suggestion, spontaneous remission, misplaced records and the like. And finally one can set oneself to take at least the first step towards an evaluation of these puzzling phenomena.'

He adopted the last and narrowed his 'quest to a search of a few cases—or a single case where the healer's art had produced an irrefutable cure'. He has to confess that up to the time of writing 'I have yet to find one "miracle cure"; and without that (or, alternatively, massive statistics which others must provide) I cannot be convinced of the efficacy of what is commonly called, faith healing.'

The Search for Medical Data

Hugh Trowell* records that he had diligently searched for any

---

* The Rev. Hugh Trowell, M.D., F.R.C.P.—formerly Senior Clinical Lecturer in Medicine, Medical School, Makerere, Uganda, in *Faith Healing*. Dr. Trowell produced for the Institute of Religion and Medicine in 1969—*Study Notes on Faith Healing*—Secular and Religious Faith Healing, Fringe Medicine and Miracles of Healing.

reports, articles or books from any of the centres of healing which described cases in a form which could be presented in the medical press. He was able to find little in these categories. He also mentions the experience of an enquiry led by the Rev. Bertram Woods (secretary of the Christian Fellowship for Psychical and Spiritual Studies)—'The investigator met with many difficulties, such as have been encountered by all those who have conducted such an enquiry. . . . In the end he found only six possible claims which could be considered a dramatic cure and "only one case was worthy of serious interview".' Dr. Trowell was asked at a later date if any new data or information had come to light which would cause him to change his view. He replied in a written communication that—'I still stand by the fact that up to the present there has been no proved well substantiated series of cases of remarkable cures, that is, cases of clearly diagnosed advanced diseases which are usually regarded in the profession as almost invariably incurable.'

Comparison with Christ's Miracles

For any case of healing to be regarded as really comparable with those of our Lord, it must meet several criteria which are common to the reports in the New Testament. The following are the chief characteristics of Christ's healing miracles:

1. The diseases and disabilities which are described in the Gospels as cured were at that time 'incurable' and most remain so today.
2. Our Lord never used means, except when He made clay on one occasion.* [The reason for its use in this case is obscure.] He usually healed by a simple word of command.
3. The cures were immediate.
4. The restoration in each case was complete, so that the preparatory question which was often used by our Lord has special significance: 'Do you wish to get well?', that is, perfectly healthy.
5. There were no recorded relapses.
6. They regularly elicited faith on the part of the person healed and sometimes in those who witnessed the healing.

A seventh feature, however, is mentioned in relation to some

* John 9:6.

of the miracles as recorded. Our Lord had 'power on earth to forgive sins' and, on one occasion, He directly related the 'sign' of physical healing to His power to forgive.*

The context in which incidents of healing are described suggests that, as compared with the prophets or the apostles, our Lord's miraculous power was unique and at first-hand, whereas theirs was by means of a delegated power and in answer to prayer. The healing was dependent upon the will of God at that time to intervene. At the gate of the Temple, Peter and John brought healing to the lame man 'in the name of Jesus Christ of Nazareth'.†

Our Lord Himself did not always wait to be asked to heal. For instance, we are not told in John 9 who made the request for healing, whether it was the man born blind or someone on his behalf. Christ apparently took the initiative and turned to him. He made clay, anointed the man's eyes and sent him to wash in the pool of Siloam.‡ Again, the man at the pool of Bethesda did not know who Christ was. There was certainly in this case no 'conditioning' of the man's attitude, but our Lord took the initiative from the start. Similarly, the man in Gadara was healed independently of his own will.§

A further fact stands out in the Gospel records. The miraculous recovery sometimes produced in the person healed a heightened spiritual perception. For example, the man born blind was granted not only natural sight, but spiritual insight. He exclaimed: 'Whereas I was blind, now I see . . . herein is a marvellous thing.'|| It would seem that when God's direct intervention brings about an act of healing, the one who is healed awakens to recognize who Jesus is and will normally acknowledge Him to be Saviour and Lord. That this was not always so was shown when nine of the lepers who were healed did not come back to recognize and thank Him.$ Our Lord called attention to their ingratitude. But, in the Gospels, most of those who were healed recognized who He was, either before or after their restoration.

---

* Matt. 9:2-6.   § Mark 5:1-17.
† Acts 3:6. || John 9:25,30.
‡ John 9:2 ff. $ Luke 17:11-19.

Chapter VII

SOME INDIVIDUAL CASES

The experience of the writers in searching for evidence has been somewhat similar to that of the other enquirers. On approaching those who have made striking claims questions are not really answered or else are deferred. This is simply a statement of fact. It is not at all intended to detract from the beliefs, sincerity or good faith of any of those involved. A request for a report on a 'series' (even if comparatively small) which were fully authenticated up to standards demanded, for example, by the Bureau de Constantations at Lourdes, would no doubt be asking far more than most centres of healing could be expected to provide. They are not geared to such requirements. But it means that sympathetic observers are compelled to confine their attention to individuals brought to their notice, and to such meagre documentation (by medically trained persons) as can be obtained. Several individual cases will be described in this chapter. The first is taken from a printed leaflet.

A Case of 'Multiple Sclerosis'

Mrs. Margery Steven of Wimborne, Dorset* has given her own account of the circumstances of recovery from a severe illness in 1960. During the Second World War, when 18, she became an auxiliary nurse at a military hospital. Subsequently, she became quarter-master of cadet-training in the occupational therapy department of a large army camp. She writes that after 5 years 'I first began to fail generally, then to lose power in a leg or arm, and then my sight became affected. . . . Gradually I got worse until 20 months ago I became so helpless (as my legs became useless) that I had to be lifted from bed to wheel chair. . . . Often my parents fed me as I had no control over the spoon. . . .

* *The Story of My Miraculous Healing* is an eight-page printed leaflet, reproducing an account broadcast on the local radio network in 1961 and subsequently reprinted, for example, in *Renewal*, No. 23 Oct./Nov. 1969.

I had no power in my left arm. My left eye was completely
closed, my right eye often had treble vision. . . About eight
months ago I started to have black-outs when I would lose
consciousness for hours. . . .' In 1954 the diagnosis was made of
multiple sclerosis and the patient was confined to her home.

Some six years later she states that: 'On February 4th 1960 I
dreamed during the night that I was sitting in a chair by my bed.
As I dreamed I thought that I put out my left leg, but I awoke
to find it was a dream. Then a voice sounded through my
room—it was my Lord's—in these words: "Tarry a little longer".
In the next few days I told several of my praying friends about
this . . . and from that moment my faith became stronger.' On
Monday July 4th—five months after the dream—she had been
lifted into and strapped into the chair as usual and the parents
left her room. 'In a matter of seconds, when I was all on my
own, my Lord Jesus healed me! I felt a warm glow go over my
body. My left foot, which was doubled up, straightened out;
my right foot, the toes of which were pointed to my heel, came
back into position. I grasped the door handle . . . undid the
straps, and said "By faith I will stand", which I did. . . . With
both parents running back into my room . . . I put out my right
arm and as I did so my left arm came out from behind me and
joined the other! . . . holding my mother's hands I stood once
more on my two feet. Then, gently putting my parents to one
side, I said "Dears, I do not need your help anymore, I'm walking
with God." Unaided I then walked from my bedroom . . . to
the kitchen. . . . Taking off my glasses I said, "I can trust God
for my hands and feet. I can trust Him for my sight." With
that, in a moment, my left eye opened and my sight was fully
restored!'

What was the local medical view of this case? Understandably
it was somewhat divided. Since there had been full reports in
the local press, her medical advisers felt free to discuss the case
with colleagues, in fact the patient was eager for this. Most of
the local practitioners took the view that it had really been a
case of hysteria.* She had, however, been diagnosed by her own

* In view of the popular use of 'hysteria', it is important to emphasise here its
original definition as a chronic psychoneurosis, characterised by a wide range of
disturbances in the motor, sensory, visual and other functions, predominantly
occurring in young women.

practitioner (after consultations with a neurologist and a psychiatrist) as having multiple sclerosis. Later, a local benefactor had subscribed the costs of a consultation in Harley Street with one of the leading neurologists of the day. A second consultant opinion had also concurred in the diagnosis of multiple sclerosis. The patient was said to have deterioriated rather rapidly, with only minor and short-lived remissions, and had then become bed-ridden. There were ophthalmic complications and cystitis. Spastic deformities developed which resulted in secondary contractures of arms, and especially of the ankles, feet and knees. After the recovery, described above, the contractures are reported 'to have vanished' (the most remarkable element in the view of a local consultant) and the wasting of the muscles was reversed (it is not clear how rapidly). The patient became fully active, subsequently doing some light nursing and local speaking. It was reported that for some twelve years* she had continued in similar light activities.

If one were to make a purely technical comment on this unusual case, it would be concerning two details in the patient's account of her symptoms. She describes treble vision in her right eye, which medically has no meaning and is, to say the least, very unusual. Monocular visual disturbance of this nature does not usually herald a disease of the central nervous system, but would rather suggest a disease of the eye itself. Also, attacks of unconsciousness are not a regular feature of multiple sclerosis. Hence, medically—so far as the published record goes—there are some unanswered questions. Also, she has at periods not been free from symptoms. But in view of the earlier recovery from her disabled condition, the patient understandably gives enthusiastic thanks to God.

Cerebral Tumour

A medical registrar from Ireland has called attention to a reported case of the healing of a cerebral tumour after prayer. The patient, who has given permission for publication, has written a full account of his experiences. At the age of 64, primarily for his angina, he was in November 1973 admitted to a medical ward in the local general hospital. Because of recent

---

* At the time of writing, the medical observers had lost contact as the patient had moved to another part of the country.

additional symptoms—very severe headaches and increasing difficulty with his balance when walking, a neurologist was brought in for consultation. After a series of investigations, including a brain scan, he was transferred to the care of a neurosurgeon at another hospital. The evidence indicated that there was 'a tumour at the base of the brain and its position was such as to make removal difficult without damaging vital structures'. 'The surgeon told my wife and elder son that I would never walk again—apparently because the nerves to the legs would be affected.' In late January 1974, the surgeon, after prior exploratory proceedings, operated and found a tumour. He said that 'he had been able to remove only a small portion' because of its position. 'At operation the tumour was found to be extensive and vascular. A little bone was removed to relieve tension.' A biopsy was not performed as the surgeon did not want to touch the vascular mass.

The patient adds: 'During the two months' period from entry to hospital, the Christians in our actively interested Baptist Church had been meeting in prayer groups almost daily on my behalf'. . . . 'After the operation all my distressing symptoms had disappeared, much to the neurosurgeon's surprise. I was instructed to report back to him in six months' time, which I did and he was more than surprised to find me so well'. . . . 'In February 1978, however, I developed double vision and, because it might have been a recurrence of the tumour, another brain scan was done. But no evidence of a tumour showed up. It was then suggested that I should go over to London to the National Hospital for Nervous Diseases, Queen's Square, which I did. They could find no trace of a tumour, but at that time (I am approaching 70) they found a circulatory problem, due to hardening of the arteries. In February 1979, being again in hospital, this time for a prostate gland operation, a further brain scan showed no trace of a brain tumour.'

Again, there are some unanswered medical questions as, for example, the exclusion of a possible cerebro-vascular disorder. Also, ample absence of a biopsy leaves the diagnosis uncertain. Since, however, the 1973 report seemed confirmed at operation in January 1974, the patient and members of his Church feel that they have grounds for their claim that the recovery was an answer to their prayers.

Chronic Varicose Ulcer

The following description of a case was received from a medical consultant in Northern England, who had discussed it with the local general practitioner who was very interested in the case. A woman in the late thirties, a leader in the youth organizations of a Baptist Church, became much limited in her activities by a chronic varicose ulcer. This was situated over the medial aspect of the right lower tibia. 'She herself did not feel free to ask for prayer in the Church for this, but a request was made by a friend on her behalf. Accordingly at a meeting in the home of one of the Church members prayer, with the laying on of hands of those present, took place. The ulcer had been present for years, with varicose eczema, and the dressings had always stuck. The following morning the patient found that the dressing had fallen off and the ulcer had healed save for one small area.' 'Over the following week-end a girl who had been present at the prayer meeting and had felt that she, too, ought to have taken part in the laying on of hands, but had held back, felt conscience stricken. She was taken to the house for this purpose, whereupon the final area healed.'

Later, the ulcer was described as 'completely healed' by a deputation of three Christian doctors practising in the area, who together examined the skin-area affected. They stated: 'That part of the leg was some $1\frac{1}{2}$ inches narrower than the contralateral one, evidence of the great tissue destruction that had taken place, but there was no evidence of the former varicose eczema and the ulcer was replaced by "the healthiest skin on the whole leg".' Despite the potential effects of the past and present treatment, the medically trained observers were convinced that something medically unusual had taken place in this case.

The Complication of Accompanying Therapy

A difficulty of clear-cut decision about the diagnosis and the medical facts relating to the course of a disease in some of the reported cases arises from the fact that treatment has already been given. Again and again, for example, it is found that in cases of advanced malignant disease there has been—before the claimed cure—a full course of radio-therapy or chemotherapy. A history, which puts the medical observer on his guard, tends to lead a layman to think that this reserve is just a matter of attempt-

ing to explain away a 'miracle'. There are several fields where
an experienced medical observer—having seen surprising
recoveries quite apart from any suggestion of a religious faith—
cannot help being cautious, where the layman has no doubts.

A recent case fully illustrates such difficulties. At a Church,
where healing services are frequently held, there was thanksgiving
for the 'complete cure' of a member, who had for some time been
suffering from bouts of abdominal pain and had come during a
'Healing Mission' to be prayed for, before going into hospital for
extensive surgery. His interest aroused, a younger surgeon (who
is a member of this same Church and who is on the staff of the
same hospital) obtained the patient's consent to discuss this event
with the surgeon concerned. The latter explained that it had
been with great reluctance and only because of the continued
insistence of both the patient and his general practitioner that he
had done a laparatomy—to find nothing but 'a very mobile
colon'. The operation was followed by no more pain, and the
patient and Church rejoiced at 'the miracle' and the fact that on
operating the 'surgeon had found nothing wrong'.

Subsequent to this 'healing', however, the patient has had
increasingly severe and frequent attacks of migraine.

Viral Meningo-Encephalomyelitis

In 1955 an active member of a Presbyterian Church in North
London, who was also a member of the staff of a well known
Christian society, took to bed with what appeared to be the onset
of a severe attack of influenza. On the second day, she had
become semi-comatose and was then found to have extensive
paralysis of the limbs, which continued to worsen. She was
admitted to what was then the Hampstead branch of the Royal
Free Hospital as a suspected case of poliomyelitis. Her condition
continued to deteriorate and the minister of the Church when he
visited the patient was not recognised. On the following
Saturday, the medical superintendent at the hospital, who had
arranged to see the minister, commented—'She is no longer in
our hands, she is in yours!'

The following day, at the end of the main prayers during the
Sunday morning service, the minister briefly stated the position
and asked the congregation unitedly to pray for this member of
their Church during a two minute silence. After the service the

minister called at the hospital. He was accompanied by one of the elders, who is medically qualified and has subsequently been appointed a professor of medicine. On their arrival at the hospital the medical staff on duty indicated that they thought that they were really wasting their time in seeing her. Whilst, however, the elder was discussing the case with a senior member of medical staff, the minister stepped into the side-Ward and offered a brief prayer. To the surprise of the staff during the afternoon and evening of that Sunday there was improvement and a slow—but ultimately complete—recovery took place over the following weeks. Subsequently the patient stated that her first conscious recollection on that Sunday was 'the sound of her minister's voice in prayer'.

It must be said that, from a medical point of view, the progress of severe infectious disease is frequently quite unpredictable. Nevertheless we would agree that this minister and his congregation were right to put their trust in God and, subsequently, to give thanks for what they believed to have been His intervention in prolonging the usefulness of a life, which has been devoted to His service.

A Compound Fracture of the Pelvis

The Evangelical* Sisterhood of Mary, Darmstadt, have described how 'a sister fell through a freshly cemented floor in the second storey of a building in course of construction landing on to the edge of a piece of lumber. On being taken to hospital an X-ray showed a compound fracture of the pelvis. The Sisterhood held 'a day of fasting, repentance and prayer, and a night of prayer'. The Mother Superior states that in 'obedience to God's commands we took the sister home ... with trembling hearts ... for according to medical advice she should have remained in traction for several weeks. We were taking her home after only two days. I had to sign for her release, accepting full responsibility. The doctor in charge spoke very earnestly to me. "Mental sickness may perhaps be healed by prayer, but prayer will never mend a broken bone," he warned me strongly.'

'At home Mother Martyria and I laid our hands on the sister and prayed. Some of the other sisters stood by and praised the victorious name of Jesus. The sister stood up from her bed. She

* That is "Lutheran".

had not even been able to move on her bed without excruciating
pain, and now she could actually stand on her feet. . . .   Then we
bowed in wonder and adoration before God—a God who indeed
works miracles. . . !   Within two weeks the sister was completely
healed, and presented herself to the doctors.'*

There have been a number of such published accounts of the
aftermath of accidents resulting in serious bone injury.   As in the
case described above, however, it could have been a fracture
of the crest of the ilium (non-weight bearing) which would have
allowed the patient to stand.   No doubt an experienced orthopaedic surgeon could comment on these cases to show the relevance
of the changes which have taken place over the years in the medical
profession's attitude to orthopaedic treatment.   But the point here
is that, in the various cases which have been cited, those concerned
'acted in faith' and see in the recovery of the patients the hand of
God at work and give Him the praise.

Epilepsy

The following is another example of the constant difficulty of
securing evidence uncomplicated by the simultaneous application
of standard medical treatments.

A vicar in the East of England, at whose Church healing
services are regularly held, refers to cases of epilepsy as having
been healed.   'My own mother was cured of epileptic fits through
the laying on of hands in 1975.   They had not been medically
controlled since 1973 and were increasing in frequency.   They
ceased suddenly after the healing service.   The neurologist is
convinced that there is no ordinary medical explanation for this
healing, but not unnaturally is not prepared to stop the drug
treatment until 3 years after they have ceased.   If you approach
us in ————— he might be willing to help in completing the
case history.'   A recent enquiry indicated that there had been no
recurrence of the epilepsy, but also that the neurologist—on
medico-legal grounds—was unwilling to agree to the cessation of a
maintenance dose of the prescribed drug.

We Need to be Sure of the Facts

Many additional reports—lay and medical—of individual cases

* *Realities. The Miracles of God Experienced To-day.* Basilea Schlink. 1975.
Lakeland.

could be given. Few of them, however, are free from questions which medically qualified observers would like to ask. In some, two strong impressions are left on a medical reader's mind:

The first is that there are comparatively few cases where the evidence is not complicated by accompanying medical treatment, Some of the latter has been prolonged. There are, also, comparatively few cases which fall into the categories of those conditions which show clearly a serious pathological condition of an organ which lends itself to the study, or is a physical disease which is almost invariably fatal, or in which there are no parallels of healing in ordinary medical experience.

The second impression is that the lay accounts of the initial clinical conditions, diagnosis and subsequent course of the disease are often considerably at variance from what the family doctors and specialists say they had actually found. Even more divergent may be what the consultants and nursing staffs actually said to the patient as compared with what the latter or his relatives (influenced no doubt by wishful thinking) thought that they said.

Two illustrative examples may be offered. Several years ago a bishop, who is high in the leadership of an overseas national Church, had entered hospital for the surgical removal of a lymphoma. Some years later there were indications of a possible intra-abdominal recurrence. The seriousness of the position became rather exaggerated amongst the diocesan clergy closest to the bishop and the size of the new growth began to be rather imaginatively described. Shortly before surgery a 'healing service' was held. Laparotomy, however, showed that no further surgery had been indicated. The 'disappearance', however, of the non-existent 'mass' was described—in print—as a miraculous answer to prayer.

Later when the surgeon concerned in the original operation was authorised by the bishop to give his opinion, he reported realistically that 'There is no mystery. The bishop had had amoebiasis in the past. ... Later there was some question whether an X-ray showed that the caecum was indented by a retro-peritoneal mass, and opinions differed whether it could be felt. At length, one of our general surgeons carried out a laparotomy. The caecal region was found to be normal and no other pathological condition was found in the abdomen.'

In *Talking Point* in the *Life of Faith** part of a letter was published
describing what (from the writer's point of view) was a miracle.
'A prayer meeting was held at my home, at the close of which a
number of us felt constrained to lay hands on a fellow member for
healing. A week or so previously he had had an X-ray of his
throat and a lump was discovered. A few days after the meeting,
on an appointment to visit the specialist, the lump could not be
found. Our friend was nevertheless admitted to hospital for
operation, with still the same result. The specialist saw him
once more, discharged him, completely baffled. . . . The X-ray
will give the medical evidence for healing.'

With the consent of the patient an approach was made by a
practitioner to the patient's own practitioner. This, however,
revealed a medical picture which was considerably different.
Complaining of difficulty in swallowing, a hospital appointment
and radiological investigation had been arranged The
radiologist's report read—'There is a moderately large sliding
hiatus hernia with free gastro-oesophageal reflux. In addition,
there seems to be a filling defect on the left in the region of the
pharynx. However, the pyriform fossae appear normal. This
could possibly be due to an epiglotic cyst. I think an examination
by an E.N.T. surgeon would be of value. The stomach and
duodenum appear normal.' The E.N.T. surgeon stated that
nothing abnormal could be demonstrated. It was later reported
that the patient, following the suggested treatment (though he
still has some mild symptoms) had been much better. He was
keeping to small well-masticated meals and taking antacid tablets.
From their day-to-day work most practitioners could no doubt
provide similar illustrations of the difficulty of accurately assessing
such cases. The total result of repeated experiences of this kind is
to pose the question—'Is it possible amidst the usual conditions
of medical practice to obtain an optimum case where all scientific
questionings can be satisfactorily answered, accompanied by the
appropriate controls?' The circumstances in which physical
healing of the body takes place—slow or fast—are such that they
do not easily lend themselves to the more stringent requirements
of this type of investigation.

From another point of view, a further question presents itself.
Is any good ever done for the kingdom of God when anyone—

* *Life of Faith*, 6th November, 1976.

however zealous and well-meaning—goes beyond the facts which can be substantiated and claims too much in the way of a special divine intervention? Would it not always—in such cases—be better to leave the matter open? By this, however, it is not meant that those individuals, who are inwardly convinced that God clearly answered their prayer of faith—or that of others on their behalf—should fail to give Him the praise. Pioneer missionaries have sometimes told of crises when (being far from any medical aid) they were overtaken by alarming signs of serious illness. Their urgent prayers were followed by a great sense of relief and confidence that all would be well. The various conditions from which they suffered (if correctly diagnosed) had certainly not followed their usual courses as described in the text-books.

Stanley Thomas, M.B.E., F.R.C.S.E., of the Baptist Missionary Society writes—'Typhoid infection was a common occurrence in Orissa, India, where I worked as doctor and surgeon for 30 years from 1939 to 1969. At that time we had no laboratory facilities to establish the diagnosis and no antibiotics for treatment. Usually the diagnosis presented no difficulties as the clinical picture and progress fitted the text book description.

Such a case was Chokroboti Naik, an unmarried male aged about 25 years. He came from a village where there was an epidemic of enteric and one of his brothers had already died from the disease. His was a severe infection and during the third week the condition deteriorated rapidly. It was before the days of anti-biotics and all we had was good nursing. One morning on my ward round I found him in extremis. He was cold and clammy, pulseless and with shallow respirations. I thought that there had been a perforation and I felt that the end was near. With a strong conviction that we ought to pray I gathered some of the staff together, we knelt and laid hold upon God with such fervour as I have rarely experienced before or since. After 15 minutes or so we returned to the ward and the patient was sitting up with a good colour, strong pulse and steady breathing. I was amazed and could only believe that our prayers had in some way been used for healing.

There was good reason to feel that his death would have greatly damaged the work of Mission in the area. Christians were few and young in the faith, his Church had already lost one member and was threatening to disintegrate; while Chokroboti's elder brother later became the most respected and influential leader in the whole Christian community which now approaches 25,000 and is steadily growing.'

Chapter VIII

HEALING MISSIONS
AND CENTRES OF HEALING

In the Christian press there appear from time to time reports of the outcome of Healing Missions and of work in various centres of healing. Some of the latter are hospices to which patients come for periods of residence. Books are written describing the original foundation, development and the present activities of these centres and their dedicated members of staff. Many descriptions are given of the people who have come to a particular centre and have been helped *spiritually* and psychologically. There are also references to others who have been physically or mentally relieved and, sometimes, cured.

The majority of these accounts are phrased in a layman's non-technical words, but there is no doubt about the conviction of those writing that there has been divine intervention in the healing of their guests. The fact that medically trained workers might have approached the details and described the course of events somewhat differently, should not be allowed to detract from the good done. To put it at its very lowest, if ordinary medical care and hospital technology has failed to relieve or cure these patients, and if cure or relief comes through these other channels, then may God be praised. It is even more to be desired that many of these sufferers, who hitherto through ignorance or unfortunate experiences in early life have neglected or rejected spiritual things, may find Christ, the forgiveness of sins and eternal life.

A central feature in the work of the Home of Divine Healing at Crowhurst, Sussex is said in their literature to be 'reconciliation with God' and 'the healing of Christ through His Church'. The Rev. E. Howard Cobb, the Rev. George Bennett and their successors have emphasised that 'Human beings may be used as channels, either in the way of prayer or personal ministration; but the healing is from God, through Jesus Christ, and from Him

77

alone'.* 'The central advice given is "Be still and know that I am God".' Again, it is claimed that 'the work in which we are engaged distinguishes itself from that of any esoteric kind by being stamped by the character of Christ's own presence. Healing might be laudable for its own sake, but the ministry to which our Lord calls His Church goes far beyond this . . . it proclaims the victory of Christ and expresses the nature of His Kingdom. It declares that only in Jesus does God completely save and make whole.'

The Lack of Accurate Statistics

As commented earlier, when a search is made for a series of cures of 'organic-disease' (apart from medical treatment), considerable difficulty is met in ascertaining the exact nature of the history, diagnosis and course of the conditions which have been described as 'cured'. Adequate medical follow-ups of the cases seem to be largely absent.

An enquiry to one apparently successful community received the reply from the leader: 'I am afraid that I cannot help you with case histories. The ministry of the Church doesn't work like that and God works in a mysterious way. We have letter after letter of thanks for new life given at . . . , sometimes physical.' Similarly, from an individual leader in a much publicised 'healing ministry' came: 'Through the years we have seen a number of healings though I would add, I think, nothing instantaneous of the type which you require and certainly there has been no documentation of the same. I rather tend to be one of those who don't keep records of these things.' Again, from a medical missionary, who had written of cases of healing in the Christian press, the reply was received: 'I am sorry that I am not really in a position to write up these cases for you in a scientific manner and (in the rush of the large turnover in our hospital) the records are inadequate. I am afraid that I have been rather like Mary, who "kept all these things in her heart"—thanking God for the spiritual lessons, but never bothering to get the facts down on paper.'

The sympathy of any reader who himself has been overwhelmed by the pressures of a really busy hospital day, will be with some of

* *Christ Healing*: E. Howard Cobb. 1975. Lakeland and *Miracles at Crowhurst*: George Bennett. 1970. Arthur James.

these correspondents. Allowance must also be made for those who are so practically busy in conditions which do not lend themselves to the production of records such as would be *de rigeuer* in the research department of a modern hospital. It has, however, been a disappointing experience to find how difficult it is to discover from Christian hospitals overseas clear and well documented cases of complete healing through prayer of organic disease apart from medical means.

A Report from Ireland

Of the available reports of healings in a community one of the best is a paper, entitled 'Miraculous Healing' by John Dundee. It was presented as an address at a meeting of the Christian Medical Fellowship in the autumn of 1976.* By courtesy and the cooperation of the Rev. Cecil Kerr, Warden of the Centre for Christian Renewal, he was able in a number of cases to interview and look into the case histories of 32 patients who had clearly benefited by contact with the community and its services of healing. The medical nature of the cases was as follows:

Proven Organic Disease	6
Possibly Psychosomatic	18
Drug/Alcohol Addiction	3
Psychiatric	1
Patients benefited	28
Patients better able to live with their affliction	4
	32

Two examples may be given. First was a case, which had been diagnosed as a bone cancer, in a man who had returned from Australia to die in Northern Ireland. He was carried to the service on a stretcher. During the following night the patient heard a voice saying, 'Get up and walk', which he did. He found

* *Miraculous Healing*: John Dundee, Professor of Anaesthesia, the Queen's University of Belfast.

himself also free from pain. He has returned to Australia and is said to be leading a normal life. The second was a woman suffering from a varicose ulcer, which had resisted all treatment, including admission to hospital for skin grafting. She attended the healing service, before the third skin graft, which was completely successful. Prof. Dundee's findings were as follows:

'Before commenting on these histories I must put on record that I received enormous co-operation from leaders in the healing ministry in the province. There was no evasion of questions and facilities were provided for seeing and speaking to more than 20 of the patients. In general, an analysis of the 32 patients, who definitely benefited from the 'ministry of healing', parallels that of Rose who published his book on Faith Healing in 1968 (see page 61). Only one of his 96 patients with demonstrable organic disease was cured after intervention of the healer. He recorded 5 patients who improved when healing was received concurrently with orthodox medical treatment. However, I am convinced that to all the 32 patients in the present series, participation in a healing service (or ministration in the home) was considered to be a very major factor in their improvement. All would testify that it was a wonderful experience.'

'Provided no harm results, either to the patients themselves or to others who may have misinterpreted what is happening, then we have no right to question these activities, even though it does not match up to our criteria for 'miraculous healing'. In my view more use should be made of the word *counselling* or even 'Christian counselling', as this would remove much of the mystique and place the subject in its right perspective. We must stop calling it 'healing'. Acceptance of the physical malady is important to many patients and this can often be achieved by a psychiatrist, but, when a fatal outcome is inevitable, Christian counselling is the only answer.

'My investigation of this community only revealed one undesirable incident from its "healing ministry". A middle-aged woman with proven bone secondaries from breast carcinoma was bed-ridden and racked with pain. A "miraculous" recovery followed prayer and laying on of hands in her home. I later saw her often shopping in the neighbourhood. She was cheerful and talkative about her cure and spoke at many healing services as well as becoming deeply involved in Action Cancer, a local organisation for which she did much publicity.* Her improvement lasted for 6 months after which she quickly deteriorated and died. Her inability to keep engagements for which she had been billed as speaker, and her absence from Action Cancer meetings, caused much comment and upset many people—particularly those whose faith was weak and who were not convinced that the healing ministry had much to offer them. The father of a colleague, who failed to achieve the expected miraculous cure of his arthritis, was shattered when he was told that this was due to his lack of faith. The same colleague knows a Methodist minister—a diabetic—who threw away his insulin syringe. Such excesses do occur.'

'*Conclusions*: As a result of this survey I would commend, rather than criticise, the role of the Church in healing the whole person. I failed to find undisputed evidence of miraculous healing, but I did meet patients who were improved in mind and spirit. The doctor, in the providence of God, can help the body, the psychiatrist can help the mind, and I believe in the concept that the mind can affect the actions of the body in this life and the fate of the soul eternally. The ministry of the Church (which I would prefer to call 'the Counselling Ministry') can play a major part in the healing of the whole man—not in the physiological preparation to which the medical profession is inclined to limit its ministry. Have we forgotten E. L. Trudeau's concept of what a good doctor should be able to do—"cure sometimes, relieve often, comfort always?". With increasing knowledge we concentrate on cures and less on symptomatic relief. We almost completely ignore comfort. The Church can place its priorities in the reverse order—comfort, relief and cure. Working together the ministrations of doctor and counsellor will be complementary.'

Reports from Overseas

In his book '*I believe in the Holy Ghost*', Michael Green† states (p. 177) 'There have recently been large outbreaks of healings in two cathedrals, one in Africa and one in Asia, where I have personal friends who were present and witnessed them. They tell me of thousands who came, and many who were healed of

* 'It is not known if she had been medically put on steroids or cytotoxic drugs during this period.'

† *I believe in the Holy Ghost*. Michael Green. 1975.

blindness, cancer, lameness and other diseases, whilst many more came to a living faith in the Saviour. The reality of this gift can only be doubted by those who are not prepared to examine the evidence.'

The cathedrals to which references are made are those of Singapore, Dar-Es-Salaam and Dodoma (Tanzania). In both the cathedrals in Tanzania the clergy reported unusual periods of mass responses to the Gospel, and a great many 'healings'. At Singapore no particular cases seem to have been followed up or could be cited by clergy or medicals to whom enquiry was made. A medical missionary, who was in Tanzania at the time, writes 'I know personally people who have been dramatically and unexpectedly healed, either through individual prayer or at meetings. But to put this in a form suitable for a medical readership is another matter. I have asked a number to try to collect data . . . but to get this from contacting scattered villagers is difficult. I know personally of a woman patient cured of attacks of asthma, and a child very ill and at point of death from a virulent enteritis, who recovered dramatically when the praying team went to the house. There have been similar unexpected recoveries.'

The services in Tanzania, to which reference is made above, were mostly conducted by the African Evangelist Mr. Edmund Sepeku. One of the African Canons reported: 'On 15.11.74 Mr. Edmund Sepeku prayed for 1050 patients at . . . and they were cured. Myself and my daughter, at the Primary School, were cured of asthma and we are well until today. On the same day, . . . was cured of blindness. A pastor from . . . was cured of impotence and a crippled young woman was cured, has since married and had a child. On 18.12.76 I and my colleagues prayed for 4 blind people at . . . and they now can see.' There follow lists (in 1975) of those who had been childless, and who now have children, cripples cured and, also, an epileptic and a case of leprosy. The Canon continues with further accounts: '1.2.76 we prayed for 180 sick people and they were cured. 26.12.76, we had open prayer and the sick were cured. 21.1.77 we prayed for people with devils and they were cured. 1.5.77 we prayed for the sick and they were cured. I have not done so since.'

One of the African Bishops describes his view: 'The healing service of Edmund Sepeku was certainly impressive. Many cripples threw away their crutches, many were able to see again, some were healed of other illnesses, especially of nervous diseases and very many "possessed" were restored to sanity. So far as I know none were examined by doctors afterwards. Many had had medical attention but with no result before the healing service, but we have no "clinical data" about them.'

But (and this is not included in any way to detract from any of the spiritual results of the remarkable Evangelist Edmund Sepeku), there is another side of the reports. The following was received from a well-qualified and experienced African doctor, who knows well the tribal areas concerned. 'During my career in this country, from 1944, there have been many reported healings, particularly in the areas on both sides of Lake Nyasa (now called L. Malawi). The 1973 outbreaks in the Dar-es-Salaam area was the only one which I have heard of, outside the Lake Nyasa area. All the outbreaks I have come across have followed the same pattern, i.e. tremendous popularity initially, with thousands of people being attracted to the meetings, followed by gradual thinning out of the attendances. When the popularity has waned, the outbreak ends and the organizer moves to another area. My own impression is that there is nothing to these healings and that the initial popularity of the meetings decreases as the actual results become known. I have not come across a single case of undoubted cure, proved by a medical examination of the clinical condition before and after the alleged healing.'

The Reports of Some American Healing Ministries

Because of the availability of their books, as cited below, it will be unnecessary to report at length the large numbers of healings claimed in North America.* In the case of Miss Kathryn Kuhlman there are what appear to be unexpected healings of many types of disease. In the view of some observers, who appear to be reliable witnesses, there have been a number of cases which cannot be lightly dismissed as due to the exaggerations of over-enthusiasm. A great many people appear to have been helped spiritually, psychologically, and also psycho-somatically. Whilst, apart from experienced local medical corroboration, there cannot

* *Nothing Impossible with God*: Kathryn Kuhlman. 1974. Oliphants, 116 Baker Street, London, W1M 2BB. (Other books by Kathryn Kuhlman are *I believe in Miracles* and *God Can Do It Again*.)

be reasonable certainty concerning the reported cure of cases of advanced 'organic' disease, there do seem to have been a sufficient number of these at least to resemble the proportional numbers which are certified by the Medical Commission as having taken place at Lourdes.*

There are seemingly reliable North American witnesses who confirm the claims for the widespread *spiritual* impact of Miss Kathryn Kuhlman's services and broadcasts. She herself says 'My guests on my weekly T.V. programme, *I believe in Miracles*, have included medical doctors and bartenders, famous educators and little children, fashion models and housewives. All have been touched by Jesus in a special way and testify of changed lives.' The independent records and books cite a variety of cases. In Miss Kuhlman's book *Nothing Impossible with God* are twenty autobiographies, which relate healings from (amongst others) inoperable malignant growths of the prostate and hip (in a child), congenital dislocation of the hip, leukaemia, cases of advanced arthritis and drug addiction.

A Critical View of Miss Kuhlman's Work

Around the year 1974, the American surgeon William A. Nolen—author of *The Making of a Surgeon* and *A Surgeon's World*—set out to examine the message and methods of Miss Kuhlman. Although a Roman Catholic he enrolled to be one of the helpers at one of her great meetings for healing. He had seen in *Time* magazine that she had healed hundreds (sometimes thousands) and that 'at least some of these cures were medically documented'. So he trained as an usher to serve in the Medical Emergencies Room and was present at a great healing service in one of the largest auditoriums in Minneapolis. He was able to observe the training of the helpers, the whole of the procedure in the meeting, to see Miss Kuhlman immediately afterwards and subsequently to interview a number from her list of those believed cured. From initially being wholly open to being impressed by the work and ready to accept all substantiated healings, he became appalled at the very small number of even *claimed* cures in proportion to the numbers of seriously ill people disappointed.

He gives an account of his impressions in pages 39-94 of *Healing*:

* See pages 59, 60.

*A Doctor in Search of a Miracle.** He states—'I had mixed emotions about the follow-up study. On the one hand I felt that Kathryn Kuhlman was a sincere, devout, dedicated woman, who believed fervently that she was doing the Lord's will. I did not want to hurt her. On the other hand, I was not sure that whatever good Miss Kuhlman was doing was not far outweighed by the pain she was causing. I could not get those crippled and idiot children and their weeping, broken hearted parents out of my mind (and all the others cruelly disappointed). . . . This brings me back to Kathryn Kuhlman's lack of medical sophistication—a point that in her case is critical. . . . I do not believe she is, consciously, dishonest. . . . I think that she sincerely believes that the thousands of patients who come to her services every year and claim cures are, through her ministrations, being cured of organic diseases. I also think—and my investigations confirm this—that she is wrong . . . *res ipsa loquitur*—"the thing speaks for itself".'

Dr. Nolen began his search with goodwill and in anticipation of another result than he found, and wrote his report with great regret. He could find no cases of the cure of proved organic disease, and became distressed at the thousands of seriously ill people who crowded service after service, only to go away bitterly disappointed.

Francis MacNutt's Claims

The books of Francis MacNutt similarly refer to considerable numbers involved in his healing services.† After describing his first case of healing in response to prayer, he adds: 'Since then I have seen many people healed—especially when I have prayed with a team or in a loving community. Although I travel too much to be able to follow up and estimate accurately, I would make a rash estimate that about half of those we pray for are healed (or are notably improved) of physical sickness, and about three-fourths of those we pray for are healed of emotional or spiritual problems.'

Describing a journey in S. America he states 'One Dominican missionary reported that nearly 80% of the poor people who

* *Healing: A Doctor in Search of a Miracle*: William A. Nolen. 1974. Fawcett Publications.

† *Healing*: Francis MacNutt. 1974. Ave Maria Press and, by the same author, *Power to Heal*. 1977.

prayed for healing in the barrios of Bolivia, where he works, were cured or notably improved.' MacNutt also quoted David Wilkerson, author of *The Cross and the Switchblade,** as saying that he has evidence that 'more than 70% of the addicts who have submitted to his programme of prayer have come off drugs and stayed off—compared with the less than 5% rate of cure in the federal hospitals.'

The Results from Lourdes

Lourdes has already been briefly discussed (p. 59). More recent information of the extent of the work and effectiveness of the shrine is relevant to these aspects of our enquiry. A recent booklet† by a qualified Roman Catholic doctor gives a few additional figures. The normal population of Lourdes is about 10,000 (but between April and October each year the visitors vary between 40,000 and 120,000 on any day). These visitors, of course, include many spiritual 'pilgrims' and not all of those visit the grotto.

Four years after the Commission was set up in 1858, seven reported miraculous cures were accepted and thirty more rejected for lack of sufficient evidence or because explicable 'by the laws of nature'. It is important to note that many 'cures' do not come to the Medical Bureau for proper investigation. 'The late Dr. Leuret, until his death President of the Bureau of Scientific Studies, estimated that (since 1858) 1,200 could be reckoned as beyond the power of nature to effect, even by modern scientific standards. Since 1920, two hundred and fifty have actually been registered at the Bureau.' The importance of these figures is that, on average, the Medical Bureau tends only to accept 6 or 7 cases a year, which in proportion to the total numbers involved is small.

Comment

The total impression made by the reports from healing centres is that their main influence is 'spiritual' rather than physical. A number of the cases in the reports are those who (by their illness and disability) have been compelled to think more deeply on the

* *The Cross and the Switchblade*: David Wilkerson. 1967. Hodder & Stoughton.
† *Lourdes*: Noel C. Hypher. 1977. Catholic Truth Society.

uncertainties and frailties of human life, and have returned to a childhood's faith or have effectively discovered the Christian religion.   There are also many for whom spiritual recovery and new insights into the realities of life have brought—as secondary effects—a psychological revolution in their outlook with resultant impact on their disabilities.   There have also been many cases where spiritual renewal has enabled the sufferers to cope more successfully with their crippling conditions.   In others, the forgiveness of sin and new birth through Christ has led—as a consequence—to greater attention to hygiene with its direct and indirect benefits.   Hence, the more easily substantiated favourable results are mostly—as one would expect from the very *raison d'etre* of the Christian Church—*spiritual* and *moral*.   It is also note-worthy that a number of the leaders in the 'Healing Ministry' are currently placing a greater emphasis upon what they call the 'healing of memories' and the 'healing of minds'.

The conclusion invites itself that there may be a small propor-tion of the cases in which God—in answer to the prayer of faith, or solely arising from the initiatives of His grace—directly heals in cases of advanced organic disease.   For reasons known only to Him, these occasions are not as frequent as many would claim and all could wish.

CHAPTER IX

CONCLUSIONS

From the mass of personal communications, reports from 'healing' institutions, booklets, paper-backs and journal articles, the task of accurate assessment has been more difficult than had been anticipated. A short and confident answer to the problem is not simple or possible. The best course seems to advance two sets of conclusions—the first from the Christian, and the second from the Medical, point of view.

The Christian Viewpoint

Writing as Christians, we remain convinced in our view that:

1. The Bible plainly teaches the Christian 'not to be anxious about anything, but in everything by prayer and petition, with thanksgiving, present your requests to God. And the peace of God, which transends all understanding, will guard your hearts and your minds in Christ Jesus.'* Physical disease is one of these things.

2. Those critically ill and the victims of accident are often unable fully to pray for themselves, and so it is the duty and privilege of the elders of the Church to join in prayer on their behalf. We accept Professor R. S. V. Tasker's approach to the interpretation of the passage in James 5:13-18 (see page 42).

3. Those interpreters of the New Testament, who regard the healing miracles of our Lord (and of the Apostles in the Gospels and the Acts of the Apostles) as being primarily authentications of His Messiahship seem justified. The miracles were 'signs' to Israel that He was who He claimed to be—and, later, they were a divine confirmation of the Apostles' declaration that the kingdom of Heaven had now been opened to others than Israel —that is 'to all believers'.

4. Whatever may have been intended by the double plural in St. Paul's phrase 'gifts of healings', there is insufficient evidence

* Phil. 4:6,7.

88

that these remained in action (at least in any spectacular form) after the deaths of the Apostles and those to whom the Apostles may have delegated them.

5. There is also insufficient evidence—some would put it more strongly and say that there is virtually no evidence—in subsequent Church History for 'gifts of healing' which can be considered the same as, or comparable to, those of the Lord and the apostolic generation. If there were miracles claimed in Patristic times they would seem to have been rather cases of 'exorcism' of evil spirits. Many of the Fathers seem primarily concerned to claim the power of the resurrection over 'demon possession' and in breaking down demonic barriers to the spread of the Church's witness.

6. There are, however, a number of isolated accounts— particularly during eras of reformation and widespread spiritual revival—of unexpected recoveries in response to 'the prayer of faith' from serious illness and the physical results of persecution. Whilst not all of these accounts are supported by as much con- temporary evidence as we would have liked, some seem to be substantiated by reliable witnesses.

7. In trying to assess the widespread international claims of the Pentecostal and 'Charismatic' Movements, the writers believe it best to approach these phenomena as something distinctly modern. It *could* be that God has done, and is doing, something *new* in His Church towards the close of the Twentieth Century. The writers accept that God in His wisdom could, at any time, use His power in a manner different from that in which He has acted in earlier times. They do not, however, believe that—except that all healing comes from God—it is a right interpretation of the New Testament to say that today's phenomena of healings are 'the same as' those of our Lord.

On the other hand, a careful perusal of the many reports of contemporary 'healings', often substantiated by witnesses whose reliability cannot be doubted, suggests that there are from time to time recoveries from serious illness and disability in answer to the prayer of faith. Such reports are the more attractive and im- pressive where our Lord is kept in the centre of interest.

8. Further, it must be said, that there is one feature which counsels caution to those who make wide claims and that is the comparative rarity of the case which can really be compared with those recorded in the Gospels. Most modern cases do not have

the same marks of immediacy and completeness conveyed by the
'straightway' (A.V.) or 'immediately' (N.I.V.) of St. Mark's
Gospel.

9. Whilst God *does sometimes heal miraculously*, as a result of the
confiding trust of His people and the corporate intercessions of
the Church, there is no room for presumption in these matters.
God heals as, and when, He pleases.

From the Medical Viewpoint

Writing from the point of view of those medically trained, there is
a need for greater reserve in accepting many of the claims.   It
may be that it will rarely be possible for any case to be presented
in a form which can meet all the scientific criteria which would
be required by a clinical research department.   A full history and
adequate details of the case, with an assured diagnosis preceding
the time of the healing, is most often lacking.   The exclusion of
the effects of any accompanying course of medical treatment and
other adjuvant favourable influences also can seldom be complete.
Finally, a long-term follow up is most often lacking, or incomplete.

At the risk of appearing scientifically sceptic or agnostic, it
seems that two things should be said:

1. The advertised 'Healing Missions' appear to make a considerable contribution to the lifting of the sum of human
   suffering amongst those affected by what may be broadly
   termed 'psycho-somatic' illness.   The lay descriptions of the
   cases claimed as healed more often than not suggest relief from
   various 'functional' states which up to that time may have
   defied ordinary medical treatment.   If this relief proves
   permanent, then it must be welcomed by all concerned as a
   real gain.   (Certainly it will be a gain for the overcrowded
   and busy outpatient departments of the hospitals!)

2. The number of serious 'organic' cases which qualify for
   acceptance as being cured by faith and apart from medical
   means, appear comparatively and surprisingly to be very small.
   Whilst it might seem to some that the criteria required by
   medically trained persons, as for example by the Medical
   Commission at Lourdes, is too strict, yet it is no more demand-
   ing than any hospital medical research 'team' would need to
   be in their ordinary scientific work.   Indeed it is doubtful if

such a team, in relation to the contemporary cases (as commonly reported), would be prepared to accept any larger proportion
of the total claimed cures, than do the medical authorities at
Lourdes, if as many. The conclusion forced on the medical
observer is the necessity of caution in making, and receiving,
claims to 'miraculous' healing.

From the way in which a given case first comes to be noticed
(and then later reported) and because of the complex circumstances
of modern life which make it virtually impossible to exclude this
factor or that, any observer can rarely secure completely satisfying
data. It would, therefore, seem a justified conclusion that, in
most situations, it is very difficult to establish *medical* proof of
sudden organic change which indicates miraculous recovery.

Christian faith and medical training can, however, happily
unite at many points. They are alike dependent upon the divine
providence, both for the normal responses of the immunological
and repair systems of the human body, as well as for any intervention of divine grace in expediting these processes at any given time.
The peace of mind and hygienic living which tend to be secondary
effects of the Gospel are considerable adjuvants to health and
longevity. As St. Paul says 'Godliness with contentment is great
gain'.*

* I Tim. 6:6.

EPILOGUE

A poignant aspect of this subject must not be omitted. In a book entitled *Notes on Spiritual Healing** a former Bishop of Durham raises in an acute form the obverse side of the widespread claims which are made for healing missions. He asks about the state of mind of the vast numbers who receive no relief and who are left either to blame themselves for their lack of faith, or to wonder secretly at God's apparent favouritism. He ends: 'Suffering saddens and perplexes, but it does not alienate us, for under the bitter covenant of pain we all must live and He suffers with us; but the partiality of favouritism, which grants exemptions from the general curse, not on any intelligible principle or in the service of any adequate case, but by mere caprice at this shrine, or at that man's hands, alarms and revolts us. Not the credit of churches, but the character of God is the issue at stake in this controversy. "Shall not the Judge of all the earth do right?" '

In bringing these pages to a close, the writers wish to affirm again their belief in the sovereignty of God who, in a world of His own creation and sustaining, is necessarily free to act in human affairs as He wills. That He evidently works miraculously at particular times for a particular purpose is clear from a reading of the Bible. If, however, it be the will of God that physical healing in answer to prayer shall not take place in any given case, the redeeming power of Jesus Christ is not thereby diminished; for the plain teaching of the gospel is that the believer will hereafter assume a body made perfect after the fashion of the resurrection body of Christ, who 'by the power that enables Him to bring everything under His control, will transform our lowly bodies so that they will be like His glorious body'.† 'For the perishable must clothe itself with the imperishable, and the mortal with immortality.'‡

* *Notes on Spiritual Healing*: H. Hensley Henson. 1925. Williams & Norgate.
† Phil. 3:21.
‡ I Cor. 15:53.

APPENDIX I: OUR LORD'S MIRACLES OF HEALING

(a) Individual Healings in the Gospels.

Person	Condition	Matt.	Mark	Luke	John
The Nobleman's son	At point of death				4:46-54
The man with unclean spirit	Demon possession		1:21-28	4:31-37	
Simon's mother-in-law	The great fever	8:14-15	1:29-31	4:38-39	
Patient with Leprosy	Leprosy	8:1-4	1:40-45	5:12-16	
Man borne by four friends	Paralysis	9:1-8	2:1-12	5:17-26	
Pool of Bethesda	Paralysis				5:2-18
Man at synagogue	Withered hand	12:9-14	3:1-6	6:6-11	
Centurion's servant	Paralysis	8:5-13		7:2-10	
The widow's son	Died			7:11-17	
The Two at Gadara	Demon possession	8:28-34	5:1-20	8:26-35	
Woman in crowd	Menorrhagia	9:20-22	5:25-34	8:43-48	
Jairus's daughter	Died	9:18-26	5:21-43	8:40-56	
Two men in house	Blind	9:27-31			
Dumb man	Demon possession	9:32-34			
Syro-Phoenician woman's daughter	Demon possession	15:21-28	7:24-30		
Man in Decapolis	Deaf and Dumb		7:32-37		
Man at Bethsaida	Blind		8:22-26		
Boy disciples could not cure	Epilepsy	17:14-21	9:14-19	9:37-43	

Person	Condition	Matt.	Mark	Luke	John
Man sent to Siloam	Blind				9:1-14
Man (after Synagogue)	Blind, dumb and demonaic	12:22-30		11:14-26	
Woman in Synagogue	Kyphosis 18 years			13:11-17	
Man	Dropsy			14:1-6	
Lazarus	Died				11:1-44
Ten Patients	Leprosy			17:11-19	
Bartimaeus	Blind	20:29-34	10:46-52	18:35-43	
Malchus	Severed ear			22:50-51	

(b) Healings of Groups and Crowds

Descriptions of Groups	Matthew	Mark	Luke	John
At Peter's door—many demoniacs exorcised and all sick healed	8:16	1:32	4:40	
Demons exorcised		1:39		
Multitudes near Capernaum—pressed on him	12:15	3:10		
Galilee—Few sick people healed	13:58	6:5		
Whole neighbourhood, villages and cities	14:34	6:55-56		
Syria—diseases, demoniacs, epileptics and paralytics	4:23		6:17	
Cities and villages, healing every disease	9:35			
Following John's question—blind, leprosy and dead	11:4		7:21	
Before feeding 5,000—healed their sick	14:14		9:11	
Galilee—great crowds of lame, maimed, blind, dumb, etc.	15:30			
Judea—great crowds	19:2			6:2

Descriptions of Groups

	Matthew	Mark	Luke	John
Great multitudes healed of infirmities			5:15	
Before Herod's threat, goes on healing and exorcising			13:32	
Blind and lame in the Temple	21:14			
(c) Descriptions of Our Lord as Healer				
'Healing every disease and infirmity'	4:23			
'Healing every disease and every infirmity'	9:35			
'Sought to touch Him . . . as many as touched'		6:56		
'Healing all who were oppressed by the devil'				Acts 10:38

APPENDIX II: BIBLICAL REFERENCES TO THE CHARISMATIC GIFTS

	I Cor. 12:8-10	I Cor. 12:28	I Cor. 12:29, 30	Rom. 12:6-8	Eph. 4:11
1.		Apostles	Apostles		Apostles
2.	Word of Wisdom				
3.	Word of Knowledge				
4.	Faith				
5.	Healings	Healings	Healings		
6.	Miracles	Miracles	Miracles		
7.	Prophecy	Prophecy	Prophecy	Prophecy	Prophecy
8.	Discerning of spirits				
9.	Languages	Languages	Languages		
10.	Interpreting languages		Interpreters		
11.		Teachers	Teachers	Teachers	Teachers
12.		Helpers		Helpers	
13.		Administrators			
14.				Servants (Deacons)	
15.				Exhorters	
16.				Financial Donors	
17.				The Merciful	
18.					Evangelists
19.					Shepherds (Pastors)

APPENDIX III

HEALINGS PERFORMED THROUGH APOSTLES
AND OTHER DISCIPLES

A. *In the Gospels*:

The Twelve commissioned and sent	Matt. 10:1-8; Mark 6:7-13; Luke 9:1-6
The Seventy commissioned and sent	Luke 10:1-20

B. *In the Acts: Healing of Individuals*:

Man at Beautiful Gate of Temple—lame	Acts:	3:1-13
Restoration of Paul's sight		9:10-19 (22:11-13)
Aeneas—paralysed		9:32-35
Tabitha—raised from dead		9:36-42
Lystra—the cripple		14:8-18
Philippa—Slave girl—spirit of divination		16:16-18
Eutychus—raised from dead		20:7-12
Paul—snake-bite healed		28:3-6
Publius' father—fever and dysentery		28:8

C. *In the Acts: Healing of Groups*:

'Many wonders and signs'	Acts:	2:43
In the streets—many sick and afflicted healed		5:12-16
Stephen—'wonders and signs'		6:8
Philip—many possessed, many paralysed and lame		8:5-8
Paul and Barnabas—signs and wonders		14:3
Paul—'extraordinary miracles—handkerchiefs, touching sick and possessed of evil spirits'		19:11-12
Malta 'rest of people who had diseases'		28:9

APPENDIX IV

BIBLIOGRAPHY

Publications on the subject of Healing have grown so numerous in the
last few years that it is not easy to keep pace with all aspects of contemporary thinking on the subject.   It has also become more difficult
to classify this literature accurately and satisfactorily.   It is hoped
that the following broad divisions, with the books listed in date order,
will prove of some service to the reader:

I   Joint Doctor-Clergy Studies

II   Individual Theological and Medical Studies

III   Biblical Studies (Concerning Spiritual Gifts and the Problem
of Pain)

IV   Roman Catholic Centres and Viewpoints

V   Literature of the Contemporary Charismatic Movements

VI   Some Useful Booklets and Articles

VII   Spiritualist and Other Healers

The books marked with * are of special value for reference purposes.

I. *Joint Doctor and Clergy Studies*:

*1910   *The British Medical Journal* of June 18, 1910.   London: B.M.A.
is devoted to Faith Healing with contributions from prominent
members of the Profession.

1910   *Medicine and the Church.*   Edited G. Rhodes.   London: Kegan
Paul.   Contributions from senior members of the Profession
such as Sir Clifford Allbutt, Stephen Paget, etc.

1914   *Spiritual Healing*: Report of Committee of Clergy and Doctors.
(By nine Clergy and eleven doctors).   (Anglican) Church
Information Office.

*1956   *Divine Healing and Co-operation between Doctors and Clergy.*   A
Report by the B.M.A. to the Archbishop's Commission on
Divine Healing.   British Medical Association.

*1958   *The Church's Ministry of Healing.*   A Report by a further Com-
mittee of 12 Medical practitioners and 12 clergy, set up by the
British Medical Association to report back to the Anglican
Archbishop's Commission.   (Anglican) Church Information
Office.

*1958 *Commission on Spiritual Healing.* A Report by the Church of Scotland Commissioners. Church of Scotland Offices.
*1962 *Religion and Medicine.* Edited by John Crowlesmith for the Methodist Society for Medical and Pastural psychology. Epworth Press.
1965 *The Healing Church*: Report of the Tubingen Consultation 1964 World Council of Christian Churches.
*1969 *Faith Healing*: Study Notes edited by Hugh Trowell for the Institute of Religion and Medicine.
1970 *Health is Wholeness*: Report of the Limuru Conference (Kenya). Edited: Dr. John Wilkinson. Protestant Churches Medical Association, Nairobi.

II. *Individual Theological or Medical Studies*:

1909 *Body and Soul.* Sub-title: "An Enquiry into the Effects of Religion upon Health, with a Description of Christian Works of Healing from the New Testament to the Present Day." P. Dearmer. Pitman.
*1918 *Miracles*: *Yesterday and To-Day.* B. B. Warfield. (Reprinted 1965) Eerdmais. U.S.A.
1924 *Spiritual Healing*: A Discussion of the Religious Element in Physical Health. H. Anson. University of London Press.
1925 *Notes on Spiritual Healing.* H. Henley Henson. Williams Norgate.
1927 *Diagnosis and Spiritual Healing.* F. G. Crookshanks.
1935 *The Christian Faith and Medical Science.* J. Burnett Rae.
*1935 *Healing*: *Pagan and Christian.* G. G. Dawson. S.P.C.K.
1937 *The Background of Spiritual Healing.* A. G. Ikin. Allen and Unwin.
1940 *Christian Healing*: Spiritual Healing in the Church of To-Day in the Light of the Doctrine and Practice of the Ante-Nicene Church. Evelyn Frost. Mowbrays.
1947 *Miracles*: *A Preliminary Study.* C. S. Lewis. Bles.
*1951 *Miraculous Healing.* H. W. Frost. Marshall, Morgan and Scott.
*1951 *Psychology, Religion and Healing.* L. D. Weatherhead. Hodder and Stoughton.
1954 *A Doctor's Casebook in the Light of the Bible.* P. Tournier. S.C.M.
1955 *The Bible and Modern Medicine.* A. Rendle Short. Paternoster Press.
1955 *Spiritual Healing.* D. Caradog Jones. Longmans.
1956 *Faith Healing and the Christian Faith.* Wade Boggs. John Knox Press, Virginia.
1960 *The Healing Ministry of the Church.* B. Martin. Lutterworth.
1961 *The Healings of the Bible.* N. B. Woods. Allen and Unwin.
*1963 *Community, Church and Healing.* R. A. Lambourne.

*1964 *The Pentecostals.* (A doctoral thesis.) Nils Block-Hoell. Allen and Unwin.
*1965 *Miracles.* Edited C. F. D. Moule. A Symposium of the Cambridge N.T. Seminar. Mowbray.
*1965 *The Miracles of Jesus.* H. van der Loos. Brill (Leiden).
1966 *The Church is Healing.* M. Wilson. S.C.M.
1967 *The Question of Healing.* Ed. G. W. Kirby. Victory Press.
*1968 *Healing Miracles.* M. A. H. Melinsky. Mowbray.
*1968 *Faith Healing.* L. Rose. Victor Gollancz.
*1973 *Healing and Christianity.* M. T. Kelsey. S.C.M.
1974 *Healing: A Doctor in Search of a Miracle.* W. A. Nolen. Fawcett Publications, Greenwich, Connecticut, U.S.A.

III. *Biblical Studies (Concerning Spiritual Gifts and the Problem of Pain)*

1894 (Revised 1975). *The Gifts of the Holy Spirit.* C. R. Vaughan. Banner of Truth Trust.
1898 *The Silence of God.* R. Anderson. Pickering and Inglis.
1918 (See also W. W. Warfield 1918 in Section II.)
1954 *The Ministry of Healing.* J. S. McEwen. *Scottish Journal of Theology.* Vol. 7, No. 2. June 1954.
1956 *The Epistle of James.* R. V. G. Tasker. Tyndale Press.
1959 *The Mystery of Suffering.* H. Evan Hopkins. Inter-Varsity Press.
1961 *All the Miracles of the Bible.* H. Lockyer. Pickering and Inglis.
1956 (See also C. F. D. Moule 1965 in Section II.)
1967 *The Question of Healing.* Edited G. W. Kirby. Victory Press.
1968 (See also M. A. H. Melinsky 1968, in Section II.)
*1970 *A Theology of the Holy Spirit.* F. Dale Bruner. Hodder and Stoughton.
1971 *The Paradox of Pain.* A. E. Wilder Smith. Harold Shaw, Wheaton, Ill.
1972 *Holy Spirit Baptism.* A. A. Hoehema. Paternoster Press.
1973 *Spiritual Gifts in the Church.* D. Bridge and D. Phyphers. Inter-Varsity Press.
1976 *Signs of the Apostles.* W. J. Chantry. Banner of Truth Trust.
(See also Section V. Publications of the Various Charismatic Movements.)

IV. *Roman Catholic Viewpoints:*

1891 *Lourdes: Histoire Medicale.* (*1858-1891.*) F. Leuret and H. Bon. Boissane.
   *(1957 Translation: *Modern Miraculous Cures:* A Documented Account of Miracles and Medicine in the Twentieth Century. F. Leuret and H. Bon. Farrer Straus and Cudahy, N.Y.)
1949 *Man, the Unknown.* A. Carrel. Hamish Hamilton.
1950 *A Journey to Lourdes.* A. Carrel. Hamish Hamilton.
1957 *Eleven Lourdes Miracles.* D. J. West.

*1974 *Healing.* Francis MacNutt. Ave Maria Press, Indiana.
1974 *The Ministry of Healing in the Church of England.* C. W. Gusmer. Alwin Press.
1977 *The Power to Heal.* Francis MacNutt. Ave Maria Press.

V. *Literature of the Contemporary Charismatic Movements*:

The Theological Outlook:
*1965 *As at the Beginning.* M. Harper. Hodder and Stoughton.
1967 *Divine Healing and the Scriptures.* D. R. P. Foot. Henry Walters, Worthing.
1969 *In My Father's House.* (Teaching of the Pentecostal Movement.) G. Canty. Marshall, Morgan and Scott.
*1973 *Salvation and Wholeness: Biblical Perspectives of Healing.* J. P. Baker. Fountain Trust.
1974 *Divine Healing: the Way of It.* F. Roy Jeremiah. Lakeland.
*1975 *Reflected Glory—The Spirit of Christ and Christians.* T. A. Smail. Hodder and Stoughton.

Reports of Healings and Healing Missions:
1948 *Recovery.* Starr Daily. Arthur James, Evesham.
1961 *Be Thou Made Whole.* Edited D. R. Smith (for Evangelical Divine Healing Convention). Rushworth Enterprise, Ware.
1964 *Healing Counsellors: A Christian Counselling Centre.* W. H. Kyle. Epworth Press.
1966 *Realities: The Miracles of God Experienced To-Day.* Basilea Schlink. Lakeland.
1968 *I believe in Miracles.* Kathryn Kuhlman. Oliphants.
1970 *Miracles at Crowhurst.* G. Bennett. Arthur James, Evesham.
1971 *Healing Adventure.* Anne S. White. Logos International.
1972 *Venture into Healing.* F. Roy Jeremiah. Lakeland.
1974 *Nothing Impossible with God.* Kathryn Kuhlman. Oliphants.
1975 *Christ Healing.* (Home of Divine Healing, Crowhurst.) E. Howard Cobb. Lakeland.
1976 *In His Healing Steps.* G. Bennett. Arthur James, Evesham.
1976 *On Roads to the Healing Christ.* B. Jordan. Arthur James, Evesham.
1976 *Christian Healing Rediscovered.* R. Lawrence. Coverdale House.
1977 *Heal the Sick.* R. East. Hodder and Stoughton.

VI. *Some Useful Booklets and Articles*:

1950 *The Sanctions of Christian Healing.* H. Roberts. Epworth Press.
1956 *The Nine Gifts of the Spirit:* B. F. Cate. Regular Baptist Press, Chicago.
1959 *Conversion: Psychological and Spiritual.* D. M. Lloyd-Jones. Inter-Varsity Press.
1964 *The Baptism and Fullness of the Holy Spirit.* J. R. W. Stott. Inter-Varsity Press.

1965 *Another Look at the Healing Miracles.* C. G. Scorer. *In the Service of Medicine,* No. 41, April 1965.
1967 *Contemporary Thought on Healing in the Light of the New Testament.* C. G. Scorer. *In the Service of Medicine,* No. 51 October 1967.
*1971 *The Supernatural in Medicine.* D. M. Lloyd-Jones. Christian Medical Fellowship.
*1976 *Christian Healing in the Parish.* M. Botting. Grove Books, Nottingham.
1979 *Healing—Biblical, Medical and Pastoral.* C. G. Scorer. C.M.F. Publications.

VII. *Spiritualist and Other Healers*:

1955 *The Reluctant Healer.* W. J. MacMillan.
*1956 *The Quest for Healing* (A Study of Twelve Healers). Godfrey Winn. Frederick Muller.
1956 *The Truth About Spiritual Healing.* H. Edwards.
1960 *Evidence for Spiritual Healing.* H. Edwards.
1965 *The Living Touch.* Dorothy Kevin. Hodder and Stoughton.
1965 *The Teaching of Dorothy Kevin.* Johanna Ernest.
1968 *Harry Edwards: Thirty Years a Spiritual Healer.* H. Edwards. Herbert Jenkins.

C.M.F. Publications

The Christian Medical Fellowship publishes a number of inexpensive books and booklets, which have interest for the wider public. The following are selected from the full catalogue:

ISBN 0 85111

Topic Booklets

The Dying Patient   954 9
    Robert Twycross   25p

The Overdose   965 4
    Anthony Smith   30p

Legalised Abortion   966 2
    Gordon Stirrat   30p

The Problem of Alcohol   967 0
    William McAllister   30p

Voluntary Euthanasia: Is there an Alternative?   938 7
    (Second edition, with appendix on legal position)
    Prof. Duncan Vere   £1

Healing: Biblical, Medical and Pastoral   969 7
    C. Gordon Scorer   35p

The Value of Human Life   968 9
    Harley Smyth   25p

Catalogue from:

The Christian Medical Fellowship, 157 Waterloo Road
    London, SE1 8XN

Trade Orders to: U.C.C.F. Book Centre, Norton Street, London, SE1 8XN